GREAT LIVES OBSERVED

Gerald Emanuel Stearn, *General Editor*

EACH VOLUME IN THE SERIES VIEWS THE CHARACTER AND
ACHIEVEMENT OF A GREAT WORLD FIGURE IN THREE PER-
SPECTIVES—THROUGH HIS OWN WORDS, THROUGH THE OPIN-
IONS OF HIS CONTEMPORARIES, AND THROUGH RETROSPEC-
TIVE JUDGMENTS—THUS COMBINING THE INTIMACY OF AU-
TOBIOGRAPHY, THE IMMEDIACY OF EYEWITNESS OBSERVA-
TION, AND THE OBJECTIVITY OF MODERN SCHOLARSHIP.

DEWEY W. GRANTHAM, *editor of this volume in the Great
Lives Observed series, is Professor of History at Vanderbilt
University. A former president of the Southern Historical Association and a member of the Council of the American Historical Association, Professor Grantham has written numerous
books and articles on modern American history.*

GREAT LIVES OBSERVED

Theodore
Roosevelt

Edited by
DEWEY W. GRANTHAM

Whether or not he was a great man is unimportant. It is
enough that the contributions he made to American life,
particularly public life, and the ways in which he made them
were magnificent.

—JOHN MORTON BLUM

A SPECTRUM BOOK

PRENTICE-HALL, INC., ENGLEWOOD CLIFFS, N.J.

For Clint, Diane, Laurie, and Wes

The quotation on the title page is from John Morton Blum,
The Republican Roosevelt (Cambridge, Mass.:
Harvard University Press, 1954).

A SPECTRUM BOOK

Current printing (last number): 10 9 8 7 6 5 4 3 2 1

C–13–783241–9

P–13–703233–8

Library of Congress Catalog Card Number: 74–126818

Printed in the United States of America

PRENTICE-HALL INTERNATIONAL, INC. (*London*)
PRENTICE-HALL OF AUSTRALIA, PTY. LTD. (*Sydney*)
PRENTICE-HALL OF CANADA, LTD. (*Toronto*)
PRENTICE-HALL OF INDIA PRIVATE LIMITED (*New Delhi*)
PRENTICE-HALL OF JAPAN, INC. (*Tokyo*)

Contents

Introduction

"Whoever would discover the spirit of America at the beginning of the twentieth century," wrote a professor of English at the University of North Carolina in 1908, "will find the quickest way to it through the biography of Theodore Roosevelt." [1] The North Carolina professor was a discerning observer, for the nation's twenty-sixth president, whose term in the White House was then drawing to a close, had touched the imagination of the American people as had no political leader since Abraham Lincoln. In his "untutored idealism" and "multifarious" activities, Roosevelt symbolized a national mood that was at once strenuous, confident, and moralistic. As president he dramatized the possibilities of the strong executive, and his administration became the focal point of the coalescing forces of national reform. Sensing the implications of his country's increasing industrial might, he sought to fashion policies at home and abroad that would meet the needs of a new era.

Roosevelt was an "accidental president" in the sense that he first came to his high office as a result of William McKinley's assassination in September, 1901. Yet few American chief executives were better prepared for the presidential role than the young New Yorker, who was not quite forty-three when he assumed office. Although Roosevelt had held few elective offices, he had been a Republican politician for almost two decades. During the 1890s he had achieved recognition as a reformer, and his spectacular experience in the Spanish-American War had made him a military hero. This catapulted him into the governorship of New York, a position he filled with distinction, and in 1900 facilitated his selection as the Republican party's nominee for vice-president.

Theodore Roosevelt was born in New York City on October 27, 1858, into a prosperous and well-established family. His father, a descendant of an old Dutch family, was a businessman who specialized in the importing of glassware; he was also a philanthropist and had an interest in genteel political reform. Theodore's mother, a pretty, gentle, and somewhat retiring woman, was the daughter of a Georgia planter who had prominent southern connections. The young Roosevelt was an intense partisan of the Union side in the Civil War, but in later years he frequently spoke of himself as "half a southerner." "I have always felt," he wrote one correspondent in 1903, "that my southern ancestry was responsible for much of my attitude in foreign politics."

[1] Edward K. Graham, "Culture and Commercialism," *South Atlantic Quarterly*, VII (April, 1908), 128.

1

But it was his father who had the most profound influence upon Theodore Roosevelt. The elder Roosevelt, Theodore recalled long afterward, was "the best man I ever knew." Handsome and buoyant, he was a man of great energy, strong will, and a joyful approach toward life. He was partly responsible for his son's early interest in nature, challenged the frail and asthmatic youngster to develop his body, and inculcated in him much of his own sense of moral duty and habit of *noblesse oblige.*

Despite a sickly boyhood, "Teedie," as he was called, lived a relatively happy life in the warm circle of his family. He had the advantages of private tutors, summer vacations, and foreign travel. A precocious lad, he grew up as an omnivorous reader while responding eagerly to the lure of the outdoors and succeeding in "making" himself physically strong. In 1876 he entered Harvard College for a gentleman's education. "Take care of your morals first," his father advised him, "then your health, and finally your studies." The young man acted upon this advice but still did well enough to be elected to membership in Phi Beta Kappa. Following his marriage to Alice Hathaway Lee in October, 1880, he began the study of law in New York.

The young New Yorker was not much interested in the law, however, and in the fall of 1881 he began, without realizing it, a long career as a professional politician. Because of a revolt in the Twenty-first District of New York, he was elected to the state assembly. People of his station in life in the 1880s looked down upon politics as sordid and disreputable, and Roosevelt himself disclaimed any intention of becoming a "political hack." But the young "dude's" three terms as a state legislator provided him with a thorough initiation into the fascinating game of politics, and he came to appreciate the fact that successful politicians had daily access to great sources of power in American society. In spite of his laissez-faire inclinations and his narrow views on many social questions, he became a "reformer," and he began to understand the potential role of public policy in dealing with the problems of an urbanized and industrialized society. Although Roosevelt was one of the dissidents who opposed the nomination of James G. Blaine as the Republican standard-bearer in 1884, he did not join those Mugwumps who voted for Grover Cleveland in November of that year. Two years later, he accepted the Republican nomination for mayor of New York and in his unsuccessful campaign emphasized the need for morality in municipal government.

Meanwhile, Roosevelt had become a rancher in the badlands of the Dakota Territory, which he had first visited on a hunting trip in 1883. The tragic deaths of his wife and mother on the same day in February, 1884, had encouraged the New Yorker to seek relief and adventure in the rugged country of the West. The two years he spent as a rancher and hunter in Dakota did much to familiarize him with the problems and possibilities of the American West. The region sustained his interest in the natural sciences and strengthened his respect for the man of action and his belief in the importance of individual character. Roosevelt, in the words of one historian, was "a Western spirit and natural backwoodsman." [2]

The young easterner had not abandoned politics, however. He supported Benjamin Harrison in 1888, and with the help of his close friend Henry Cabot Lodge received an appointment in April, 1889, as a member of the United States Civil Service Commission. In this position he energetically attacked the spoils system, even when it was being employed by his own party, and laid the basis for his reputation as a national reformer. He also became acquainted during his six years in Washington with most of the political leaders on the national scene. In 1895 Roosevelt returned to New York to accept appointment under an independent mayor as a member of the city's board of police commissioners. His career as president of the board was tumultuous, but his untiring efforts to make the department honest and efficient broadened his understanding of urban problems and made his name a household word in New York.

After working hard for the Republican ticket in the fiercely contested campaign of 1896, Roosevelt was rewarded with a position in the new McKinley administration as assistant secretary of the navy. Here he helped introduce certain administrative reforms, labored zealously in behalf of naval preparedness, and played a significant role in readying the Pacific fleet for its triumphant action against the Spanish in the spring of 1898. The worsening Cuban crisis provided a focus for Roosevelt's intense nationalism. Indeed, he yearned for war. He thought of war, writes one of his biographers, "in terms of man-to-man combat, dashing cavalry charges, and brilliant tactical maneuvers; not of mass carnage, germ-infested prison camps, and endless, stultifying boredom." [3] When the war finally came, he seized the opportunity to satisfy a long-time dream by becoming lieutenant-colonel of a volunteer cavalry regiment. His exploits with the Rough Riders during the brief Cuban campaign led directly to his gubernatorial victory in the fall of 1898. As governor of the nation's largest state in 1899 and 1900, Roosevelt managed to cooperate with Thomas C. Platt, the "easy boss" of New York Republicans, and at the same time to carry out a moderate reform program. He wanted to serve a second term but yielded gracefully to nomination as vice-president in 1900. His nomination was asured both by his own flattering popularity

[2] Albert Bushnell Hart, "Roosevelt as Pioneer," in Hermann Hagedorn, ed., *The Works of Theodore Roosevelt*, National Edition, 20 vols. (New York, 1926), VIII, ix.

[3] William Henry Harbaugh, *Power and Responsibility: The Life and Times of Theodore Roosevelt* (New York, 1961), p. 98.

among rank and file Republicans and by the desire of Senator Platt and other Republican leaders, for different reasons, to have him on the national ticket.

This sketch of Theodore Roosevelt's road to the White House gives little indication of the man's versatility and extrapolitical interests. He was, for example, a competent naturalist and his interest in this field remained great even after he entered politics. His steady pursuit of the strenuous life was one of the most compelling features of his experience in the 1880s and 1890s. He was also a man of letters, publishing many books and articles on ranching and hunting, history, and current affairs. In 1898 he was elected to membership in the National Institute of Arts and Letters. He found time amid these numerous activities to marry Edith Kermit Carow in December, 1886, and to become the father of six children. The Roosevelt home at Oyster Bay, Long Island, was the happy scene of outdoor activities, intellectual discourse, and political strategy.

What manner of man was Roosevelt, this president who was both an aristocrat and an intellectual? He was, for one thing, a skillful politician who had demonstrated a capacity for administrative and executive leadership. He had managed to be both a reformer and a loyal party man, steering a middle course between the spoilsmen and the Mugwumps, between political orthodoxy and independentism. An ardent nationalist, he was experienced in the metropolitan politics of the East, felt a spiritual kinship with westerners, and had some understanding of the tortured history of the South. Although his social philosophy reflected the pervasive Darwinism of the times and he applied the doctrine of the struggle and survival of the fittest to individuals and societies, his social Darwinism was softened by his sense of moral duty, by his faith in the importance of personal character, and by his feeling that evolution could be determined by a purpose outside of the process itself. He was not a Jeffersonian. But he was a great admirer of Abraham Lincoln, and there was a good deal of truth in his assertion of 1906 that "while I am a Jeffersonian in my genuine faith in democracy and popular government, I am a Hamiltonian in my governmental views, especially with reference to the need of the exercise of broad powers by the National Government." He was, fundamentally, "an institutionalist, a gradualist, a moralist." [4] By the time Roosevelt became president, he had built, in Professor John M. Blum's vivid phrase, "an eclectic intellectual home, its parts connected, but the whole more comfortable than integrated. It was designed to provide security for a man whose personality compelled him to act, whose profession required him to compromise, and whose moral beliefs forced him to justify everything he did. There was room for Roo-

[4] John Morton Blum, *The Republican Roosevelt* (Cambridge, 1954), p. 6.

sevelt's Darwinism, his social gospel, his chauvinism, and his strenuosity, and these were not tightly compartmented, but related each to the other." [5]

During his first months in the White House, Roosevelt moved cautiously. The party organization was in the hands of Mark Hanna and other McKinley men. Congress was dominated by a powerful group of conservative Republicans. The new president wanted, as he made implicit in his comprehensive annual message of 1901, "to go a little ahead of my party in the right direction, but not so far ahead that they won't follow me." His first objective was to win control of his party. This he proceeded to do, adroitly constructing a personal organization within the Grand Old Party that made his nomination certain in 1904. He was then elected "in his own right," winning by a landslide over Alton B. Parker, the Democratic nominee, and demonstrating his enormous popularity with the American people. In addition to establishing control of his party and obtaining an impressive mandate from the voters, TR also contrived his own presidential program. Although Roosevelt's policies seemed both to lack symmetry and to have an improvisational character, his program became more comprehensive as it unfolded, and the measures he advocated for the solution of the pressing problems of an industrial age frequently proved to be farsighted as well as realistic.

In the domestic sphere, where his policies met stout opposition, Roosevelt enjoyed only limited success. While recognizing the dangers of uncontrolled corporate power, he accepted the inevitability and desirability of big business. He resurrected the Sherman Antitrust Act in the prosecution of the Northern Securities Company in 1902, persuaded Congress to create a Bureau of Corporations in 1903, waged a campaign of publicity against the abuses of large corporations, and urged federal supervision of all concerns engaged in interstate commerce. He moved skillfully, in effecting passage of the Hepburn Act in 1906, to secure an orderly and effective system of railroad control. Having moderated a youthful suspicion of organized labor, he intervened spectacularly in the protracted anthracite coal strike of 1902 to get a solution that was fair to the workers. He helped secure an extension of federal authority in the enactment of a pure food and drug law, a meat inspection act, and welfare legislation for the District of Columbia. The Roosevelt administration was also distinguished for its contributions to the cause of conservation. The youthful president dramatized the need for conservation by supporting more liberal legislation, by making the Forestry Service more efficient, by adding millions of acres to the national forests and withdrawing waterpower sites and coal lands, and by creating national monuments and wild-

[5] *Ibid.*, p. 32.

life refuges. In this and other areas he increasingly saw the need, as John M. Blum has said, for "strong, disinterested government equipped to define, particularly for a powerful executive prepared to enforce, the revised rules under which the America of immense corporations, of enormous cities, of large associations of labor and farmers could in orderly manner resolve its conflicts." [6]

In the conduct of foreign affairs Roosevelt encountered fewer restraints than in the case of his domestic policies. He was determined to protect American interests abroad, wherever they might be, and he was desperately eager to have the United States play the part of a great nation on the world stage. Understanding the interdependence of nations and the way in which the world was being changed by the new technology, the twenty-sixth president was convinced that the United States could not insulate itself from foreign politics. He wanted to help create order and security among nations and to avoid what he regarded as a situation of potential chaos in international affairs. Delighting in personal diplomacy, he busied himself with the formulation and execution of strong policies in the foreign theater. He worked assiduously to develop the American navy. In the western hemisphere he resolved a dispute with Canada over the Alaskan boundary on terms highly favorable to his own country, persuaded the British to agree to the abrogation of the Clayton-Bulwer Treaty of 1850, and intervened decisively in the Caribbean by moving boldly and somewhat ruthlessly to acquire a site for an interocean canal and by broadening the Monroe Doctrine to justify an American role of policeman in Latin America. He displayed great resourcefulness in mediating the Russo-Japanese War in 1905, thereby becoming the first American to receive the Nobel Peace Prize, and he attempted to solve the problem of Japanese immigration to the United States. While Roosevelt was not very sensitive to conditions in China, which he persisted in viewing in colonial terms, he moved shrewdly and skillfully to deal with the complications growing out of Japan's new position in Asia. By the end of his administration, he had effected a *rapprochement* with the Japanese. In Europe, meanwhile, he played a part in resolving the dangerous crisis of 1906 over Morocco.

"My business," TR remarked near the end of his tenure, "was to take hold of the conservative party and turn it into what it had been under Lincoln, that is, a party of *progressive* conservatism, or conservative radicalism. . . ." Roosevelt had been less successful in this respect than he supposed. Furthermore, his record as a domestic reformer had a highly unfinished aspect, as his handling of the tariff revealed, and there were instances of arbitrary and unfair action, as in his dismissal of the Negro soldiers charged with involvement in the Brownsville

⁶ Blum, *The Republican Roosevelt*, p. 109.

affray of 1906 and his "Muckrake" speech against irresponsible journalists in the same year. There were unhappy consequences flowing from his foreign policies, particularly in the Caribbean. Some of the controversies that swirled around his strenuous presidency, including those over "simplified spelling" and "nature fakirs," seemed extraneous and pointless. But if there were flaws in Roosevelt's leadership as president and limitations in his record of accomplishments, there was also much to be said for his strengthening of the office. He had a dynamic concept of the presidency, he proved to be an able administrator, and he tried to invoke the powers of the national government to deal with crucial social problems. If his reforms were modest, they were sufficient to demonstrate his concern for a new role for government. And his leadership went a long way in reviving a sense of national purpose among Americans.

Roosevelt's control of the Republican party was revealed anew by the ease with which he chose his successor, William Howard Taft. But by mid-1910, when the Colonel returned from his celebrated hunting expedition to Africa, the GOP was bitterly divided between the conservatives, who increasingly looked to Taft for support, and the progressives, many of whom regarded Roosevelt as their natural leader. During the last years of Roosevelt's administration, when his own progressivism was growing stronger and more comprehensive, conservative Republicans had attacked him with mounting severity. He had valiantly tried to bridge the widening gap in his party, and in a measure he had succeeded. Yet the incipient party division late in TR's presidency grew rapidly in 1909 and 1910 in the wake of President Taft's political ineptness and the expanding pressures for reform in Washington. Roosevelt could not avoid involvement in the party crisis, and in 1910 he sought with all of his accustomed energy to bring harmony to the embittered Republicans. At the same time he promulgated the basic principles of his own maturing progressivism—the "New Nationalism"—a call for strong central government that would look first to national needs and place human rights above property rights.

At first Roosevelt intended to keep his own name out of consideration as a presidential candidate in 1912. Following his sweeping victory of 1904, he had publicly renounced any ambitions for a third term. By early 1912, however, the Colonel had changed his mind: events had exacerbated his resentment against Taft, he had become more convinced than ever of the need for further national reform, he was reassured as to his own popularity with the people, and he was still personally ambitious, still eager to possess power. Thus the former president "threw his hat in the ring," and when the Republican national convention denied him the nomination, despite his impressive victories in most of the preferential primaries, he led a large group of insurgents out of the GOP and organized his own Progressive party. Standing at Armageddon on a platform devoted to advanced social reforms, Theodore Roosevelt was, momentarily, the leader of a great movement. Characteristically, he waged a stouthearted campaign. He ran second to the Democratic nominee, Woodrow Wilson, and had the satisfaction of seeing Taft and his administration defeated and repudiated. But he knew that there was no future for the new party, and four years later he maneuvered to bring the remnant Progressives back into the Republican ranks. His interests by that time had shifted from domestic reforms to American preparedness and the Great War in Europe.

The final years of Theodore Roosevelt's life were his unhappiest ones. He found time for one last adventure, a perilous trip in 1913 to explore the wilds of Paraguay and Brazil. After war broke out in Europe in 1914, he soon became a zealous advocate of greater United States preparedness and a carping critic of President Wilson's foreign policy. He wanted the United States to enter war on the Allied side long before that step was taken in April, 1917, and when the decision was made he tried unsuccessfully to get command of a volunteer division for service at the front. His four sons did serve in Europe, and the youngest was killed in action, but the aging Rough Rider had to content himself by supporting the war effort at home. In a way it was his saddest hour, for he succumbed to the war hysteria and preached a doctrine of intolerant Americanism. Although his health was poor in these last years, he was widely regarded as the leading contender for the Republican presidential nomination in 1920. Had he lived to receive that nomination and win the presidency again, the politics of the 1920s might have been different. But that was not to be. "Greatheart" died in his sleep during the early morning of January 6, 1919, at his beloved Sagamore Hill. An era in American political life had ended.

Theodore Roosevelt was a prolific writer and speaker. One edition of his writings, made up of his books and a selection of his articles, state papers, and speeches, totals twenty volumes. At least 100,000 of his letters have been preserved, and a significant number of them have been published. "Being a normal human being," wrote his friend Brander Matthews, "he liked to celebrate himself and to be his own Boswell; but he was never vain or conceited in his record of his own sayings and doings. He had the saving sense of humor, delighting in nothing more than to tell a tale against himself." He had, recalled Matthews, "the kodak eye of the born reporter." [7] Roosevelt's writings

[7] Matthews, "Theodore Roosevelt as a Man of Letters," in Hagedorn, ed., *The Works of Theodore Roosevelt*, XII, xiv–xv.

revealed the enormous range of his factual information, the variety of his interests and attributes, and the extent to which his knowledge had been digested and integrated. While his style was somewhat prolix, it was nevertheless direct, robust, and clear, and it revealed a gift for narrative prose. The Colonel made it an effective instrument in dramatizing himself and his policies. His forthright expression, vivid phraseology, and picturesque denunciation of those he disliked (he called Bernard Shaw a "blue-rumped ape" and Maurice Low a "circumcised skunk") elicited continuing interest. His letters were frequently charming and threaded with humor, which no doubt explains why his *Letters to His Children* proved to be his best-selling book.

In considering Roosevelt's own view of the world and of himself, a word of caution is in order. There was a didactic element in what he wrote and said—after all, he pronounced the White House a "bully pulpit." Furthermore, the sheer volume of his written words makes it difficult not to overestimate the significance of his role. "His egotism, sense of history, and volubility," one historian has recently suggested, "led to a huge correspondence which, in its very fullness and plausibility, tends to impose Roosevelt's own pattern upon events." [8]

Yet the lineaments of the man's character and career emerge in bold relief from his own words. Nowhere else can one find so vivid an illustration of his remarkable personality. He communicated in what he wrote and said, as well as what he did, something of the intense vitality which, in Allan Nevins' phrase, "made other men look a little pallid, and that, tiring friends, sometimes tired the country." The charm and buoyancy of his personality were scarcely less dominant in his makeup, for he approached life joyously, and he possessed in abundant measure magnetism, warmth, and concern for others. He delighted in his wife and children. He had an extraordinary capacity for friendship and took immense satisfaction in bringing different kinds of people together. Endlessly curious and possessing a childlike sense of wonder, the man had a good deal of the boy in him ("You must remember," remarked one of his British friends, "that the President is about six"). Who among our presidents but TR could have written this characteristic note to one of his sons near the end of his presidency? "Do you recollect," he wrote, "how we all of us used to play hide-and-go-seek in the White House, and have obstacle races down the hall when you brought in your friends?"

Roosevelt was a complex man, and there was a more somber element in his personality. To some observers he seemed always to be acting, to be playing a role. "Ike" Hoover, the White House usher, remem-

[8] Charles E. Neu, *An Uncertain Friendship: Theodore Roosevelt and Japan, 1906–1909* (Cambridge, 1967), p. 13.

bered that the president "seemed to be forcing himself all the time; acting, as it were, and successfully." [9] The "melancholy side" to his soul revealed itself, as one of his interpreters remarks, "in his furious energy, his determination to cram his days more full than they can hold, as if life would otherwise be intolerable." [10] The result was what Gamaliel Bradford called a "lack of inwardness." But if the Colonel avoided introspection, there is little evidence that he had a troubled conscience. His self-esteem seldom flagged, and he frequently exaggerated his accomplishments. When someone suggested in 1901 that the Rough Rider had not really been at San Juan Hill during the famous charge of 1898, his response had been, "This is a good deal like saying that Pickett was not at Gettysburg." Yet Roosevelt was not without humility; he had doubts about his own capacity and consistently denied that he was a great man.

Theodore Roosevelt seemed to feel a compulsion toward duty, morality, and justice. He enjoyed work, accepted responsibility, and was willing to labor with whatever materials were at hand. While he was firmly convinced of the social value of religion, his religious creed is difficult to define. One thing is clear: he believed passionately in struggle and in the gospel of work. He once admitted that his whole religious sense could be summed up in the verse from St. James: "I will show my faith by my works." As he wrote a friend in 1901, ". . . it seems to me that in this life the best possible thing is to have a great task well worth doing, and to do it well." Conduct was important to Roosevelt, and while his views on race and religion were somewhat ambiguous, it was the character of the individual that he prized most highly. He was highly moralistic. "Over and over," wrote that observant editor William Allen White, "the theme is hammered into the mind and heart of the multitude: Be good, be good, be good; live for righteousness, fight for righteousness, and if need be die for it." [11]

A pragmatist in political matters, Roosevelt was committed to politics as the art of the possible. Having no elaborate theory of government, he performed best in dealing with concrete situations. Nothing was more central to his politics than his desire for power and his satisfaction in using it. Fearing social violence, he was obsessed with the need to impose order; for only in order could there be morality. He constantly warned of "the twin opposite dangers to be feared—the Scylla of mob rule, and the Charybdis of subjection to a plutocracy." For all his love of combat, boisterous impulsiveness, and strident rhetoric, his normal approach was one of moderation. His

[9] Irwin Hood (Ike) Hoover, *Forty-Two Years in the White House* (Boston and New York, 1934), p. 231.

[10] Edward Wagenknecht, *The Seven Worlds of Theodore Roosevelt* (New York, 1958), p. 192.

[11] White, in Hagedorn, ed., *The Works of Theodore Roosevelt*, XIII, xi.

talent as an administrator was related to his ability to profit from advice. "Prepare me a paper on the subject" was a frequent request.

Few American leaders have provoked more comment during their lifetimes and afterward than Theodore Roosevelt. No one can read through many of the newspapers, magazines, and popular biographies of Roosevelt's generation without becoming aware of the enormous influence the man exerted on his contemporaries. He communicated some of his own exuberance and *joie de vivre* to his countrymen. "His high spirits, his enormous capacity for work, his tirelessness, his forthrightness, his many striking qualities," recalled Mark Sullivan, "gave a lift of the spirits to millions of average men, stimulated them to higher use of their own powers, [and] gave them a new zest for life." [12] TR had the capacity of putting himself in the context of ordinary people, and he won the loyalty of Americans as have few other presidents. While he was able to deal successfully with all types and classes of men, his greatest appeal was to the middle-class American, whose fundamental values he instinctively shared. Roosevelt also inspired a remarkable loyalty and devotion in a large number of young lieutenants and adherents. "His mere presence was so full of vitality," Henry Cabot Lodge later wrote, "so charged with energy, which it gave forth with lavish generosity, that it was contagious, and seemed to bring all the possible joy of living as a gift or rather as an atmosphere to those who rode or walked beside him." [13]

Irvin S. Cobb once remarked that "you had to hate the Colonel a whole lot to keep from loving him." That was true. Nevertheless, Roosevelt alienated many of his contemporaries, some of whom hated him fiercely. His own intense dislike of "Mollycoddles," men "who think feebly and act feebly," of pacifists, and of the "lunatic fringe" of reform was frequently reciprocated. His self-righteousness and egotism aroused suspicions in certain quarters, and the unending controversies in which he was caught up inevitably created enemies. Many southerners condemned his appointment policies and were scurrilous in their denunciation of the notorious White House dinner for Booker T. Washington. Democratic politicians found in him a frustrating opponent, a complete and occasionally ruthless partisan who enjoyed immense popularity with the voters.

Whatever their reactions, Roosevelt's contemporaries seldom found him dull. He was in fact the most exciting and amusing public figure of his generation. It was no accident that he was a great favorite with contemporary cartoonists—and with that sage wit, Mr. Dooley. Much of his significance can be attributed to the fact that he symbolized in

[12] Sullivan, *Our Times*, 6 vols. (New York, 1926–35), II, 399.
[13] Lodge, in Hagedorn, ed., *The Works of Theodore Roosevelt*, X, xx.

his thinking and action so many of the folk attitudes of his time. After a visit to the White House in 1903, the British writer John Morley was quoted as saying, "Roosevelt is not an American, you know. He is America." The first national image of Roosevelt was that of the Rough Rider. This image was associated with the cowboy, the hunter, and the frontiersman. It was a symbol of violence and of a lingering primitivism, and it celebrated the man of action and the strenuous life.[14] TR's commitment to hard and sustained work provided another symbol and strengthened a cherished cultural concept. The Colonel's militant righteousness projected still another symbol, one that was identified with the image of the reformer, the trustbuster, the world policeman. Roosevelt also mirrored his generation's faith in progress, and he was, in Henry F. May's words, the "greatest spokesman of practical idealism in America in 1912." Finally, there was the symbol of the corrupt politician. A considerable number of Americans saw Roosevelt not as a reformer but as an opportunist and a demagogue; others viewed him as a tyrannical figure who abused the powers of the presidency. However disparate these symbols may appear, they reflected remarkably well the instincts of the country as a whole.

In 1923 Lord Charnwood published a slender biography of Theodore Roosevelt. The English writer hoped, he said, to arouse more interest in "a powerful and a noble man, whose fate it was for a considerable while to rivet and indeed fatigue the attention of civilized mankind, then to undergo eclipse, and to die when the eclipse was total. . . ." [15] Charnwood may have exaggerated the extent of Roosevelt's eclipse in the eyes of his contemporaries, but his book and a large number of other eulogistic biographies and memoirs published soon after the Colonel's death nourished the Roosevelt legend. Most of these books and articles were written by Roosevelt's friends and associates. They tended to be uncritical and to picture him as a heroic figure whose memory should be preserved.

A reaction in the general attitude toward the twenty-sixth president set in during the 1920s, and his reputation underwent further devaluation in the 1930s. H. L. Mencken, for example, ridiculed Roosevelt as a militarist and political demagogue. The former president's public role after 1914 seemed to many Americans in the twenties and thirties to cut him off from the progressive movement, to make him rather irrelevant as a source of modern liberalism. The first scholarly monographs on the Roosevelt administration—Tyler Dennett's *Roosevelt and the Russo-Japanese War* (1925) and Howard C. Hill's *Roosevelt*

[14] Roosevelt as a symbol is considered in a suggestive unpublished study by David Francis Sadler, "Theodore Roosevelt: A Symbol to Americans, 1898–1912" (Ph.D. diss., University of Minnesota, 1954).

[15] Lord Charnwood, *Theodore Roosevelt* (Boston, 1923), p. 3.

and the Caribbean (1927)—were somewhat critical of TR's policies. In 1931 critical biographies of Roosevelt by Walter McCaleb and Henry F. Pringle appeared. Pringle's scintillating book won a Pulitzer Prize and did more than any other interpretation to debunk the Roosevelt legend. Pringle saw Roosevelt as a somewhat ridiculous figure, perennially adolescent and often amusing, but hardly to be taken seriously as a major political leader. Other writers, including John Chamberlain, Walter Millis, and Matthew Josephson, helped fix the image of a president whose policies were inconsistent, whose reforms were limited, and whose thinking was superficial. Some critics detected a strain of fascism in his thought. Americans in the era of the Great Depression did not find him a congenial figure, despite the fact that part of his New Nationalism was reflected in the program and philosophy of the New Deal. While a loyal band of his followers devoted themselves to keeping his memory alive, his significance declined with the passing years, and he appeared increasingly as merely a quaint, comic, and rather frivolous figure out of the past. In 1939 Louis Filler observed that "each year Roosevelt becomes less impressive in retrospect, and it is unlikely that he will ever resume the stature he enjoyed in his days of triumph." [16]

Yet soon after this was written, historical interest in Roosevelt began to quicken, and a radically different estimate of his place in the history of American politics began to emerge. The first notable step in TR's reappraisal and rehabilitation came in 1946 with the publication of George E. Mowry's illuminating study, *Theodore Roosevelt and the Progressive Movement*. The early 1950s brought an impressive eight-volume selection of Roosevelt's letters. The appearance of the letters, with the penetrating notes and commentaries provided by Elting E. Morison and associates, did a great deal to stimulate scholarly interest in the twenty-sixth president, as did the brilliant interpretation by John M. Blum entitled *The Republican Roosevelt* (1954). Blum's book probably did more than any other work to restore Roosevelt's reputation as a leader of compelling historical significance. Roosevelt also seemed to become more relevant to Americans in the years following World War II. His *Realpolitik* did not seem out of place in a new age of international power politics. His concern for stable social arrangements and for orderly change, his efforts to reconcile conflicting interests, and his contributions to administrative efficiency appealed to the conservative mood and the consensus tendencies of the fifties. The revival of interest in Roosevelt was in part a result of a new fascination with modern history and a comprehensive investigation of the progressive era by a host of younger historians.

[16] Filler, *Crusaders for American Liberalism,* new ed. (Yellow Springs, Ohio, 1950), p. 44.

The magnitude of the historical reappraisal of Roosevelt in the last twenty-five years is large. Several new biographies have appeared. Howard K. Beale completed a major new evaluation of the Roosevelt foreign policies, and several specialized monographs have been published on various aspects of his international leadership. Scores of articles on various parts of his public career have appeared. Several new syntheses of the era he dominated have been published, as well as numerous biographies of his contemporaries and valuable studies of such subjects as conservation, business regulation, organized labor, and diplomacy. Popular writers have also found Roosevelt attractive and have contributed to the long list of historical works on the man and his times. The older skepticism about Roosevelt did not disappear altogether in this period. Richard Hofstadter and Daniel Aaron, for instance, in books published in 1948 and 1951, respectively, were harshly critical of the authoritarianism and militarism in TR's thought. (It is significant that both historians appear to have moderated their criticisms of Roosevelt since then.) Professor Beale, while sympathetic in his approach, was disturbed by the Rough Rider's eagerness for unrestricted power and by the unhappy legacies of his foreign policies. Some of the more radical American historians such as Gabriel Kolko see in Roosevelt a spokesman and sometimes a tool of the industrial and financial establishment.

Yet as a whole the cumulative interpretation of our time is a far cry from both the heroic image of the early idolaters and the irresponsible and adolescent portrait of the debunkers. Future interpreters of the inimitable Colonel will no doubt discover new meanings in his remarkable career, but his stature as a dominant figure in the first part of our modern history is now well established. Why this is true is the burden of this book.

Chronology of the Life of Theodore Roosevelt

1858	(October 27) Born in New York City, the son of Theodore Roosevelt, Sr., and Martha Bulloch Roosevelt.
1876	(September) Entered Harvard College.
1880	(June) Graduated from Harvard College. (October 27) Married Alice Hathaway Lee.
1881	(November) Elected to New York State Assembly.
1882	Published *The Naval War of 1812*. (November) Reelected to New York State Assembly.
1883	(September) Bought ranch at Medora, Dakota. (November) Reelected to New York State Assembly.
1884	(February) Deaths of Martha Bulloch Roosevelt and Alice Lee Roosevelt. (June) Delegate to Republican national convention.
1884–6	Rancher in Dakota Territory.
1886	(November) Defeated as Republican nominee in New York mayoralty election. (December) Married Edith Kermit Carow.
1889	Published Volumes I and II of *The Winning of the West*. (May) Took office as civil service commissioner.
1894	Published Volume III of *The Winning of the West*.
1895	(May) Took office as member of New York City Police Commission.
1896	Published Volume IV of *The Winning of the West*.
1897	(April) Appointed assistant secretary of the navy.
1898	(April) Accepted lieutenant colonelcy in First U.S. Volunteer Cavalry Regiment (Rough Riders). (May) Resigned as assistant secretary of the navy. (November) Elected governor of New York.
1900	(June) Nominated for vice-president by Republican national convention. (November) Elected vice-president.
1901	(September 14) Sworn in as president following President McKinley's death.
1904	(November) Elected president in his own right.
1909–10	Hunting trip to Africa and tour of Europe. Accepted Nobel Peace Prize in Christiania, Norway.
1910	(June) Returned to the United States.
1910–14	Contributing editor, *The Outlook*.

1912	(February) Announced candidacy for Republican presidential nomination.
	(August) Nominated for president by Progressive party.
	(November) Defeated in presidential election.
1913	Published *Autobiography*.
1913–14	Expedition to South America.
1914	Campaigned for Progressive party candidates.
1915–16	Leader of preparedness campaign.
1916	Declined Progressive party nomination for president; endorsed Republican nominee, Charles Evans Hughes.
1917	(April) Request to raise a division of troops for service in France rejected.
1917–18	Ardently supported American war effort.
1919	(January 6) Died at Oyster Bay, New York.

PART ONE

ROOSEVELT LOOKS AT THE WORLD

The diversity of Theodore Roosevelt's interests, the important role he played in state and national politics, and the enormous volume of his writings and speeches complicate the task of compiling a representative and illustrative selection of his own words. Yet the major aspects of his thought are not difficult to discover; his basic values and predispositions were formed early in life, and he expressed them time after time. This is not to say that his attitudes did not change with the passage of time, but rather to note the impressive continuity and consistency of his fundamental values and opinions. The selections in this part of the book are designed to set forth Roosevelt's most characteristic and significant ideas and to illuminate his own view of his evolving politics and policies.

1
"Teedie": The Formative Years

Roosevelt grew up in an affluent family that gave him a sense of security. Family tradition, most notably through the example of his father, did much to mold his basic character and to instill in him a rationale of noblesse oblige, *moral idealism, and public service. The documents included in this section touch on the young Roosevelt's family heritage and on some of the other influences that shaped his development during this formative period, including his enthusiasm for natural history.*

FAMILY

My Dear Mamma[1] I have just received your letter! What an excitement. How nice to read it What long letters you do write. I don't see how you can write them. My mouth opened wide with astonish when I heard how many flowers were sent in to you. I could revel in the buggie ones. I jumped with delight when I found you heard the mocking-bird, get some of its feathers if you can. Thank Johnny for the feathers of the soldier's cap, give him my love also. We cried when you wrote about Grand-Mamma. Give my love to the good natured (to use your own expresion) handsome, lion, Conie, Johnny, Maud and Aunt Lucy. I am sorry the trees have been cut down. Aunt Annie, Edith, and Ellie send their love to you and all I sent mine to. I send this picture to Conie. In the letter you write to me tell me how many curiosities and living things you have got for me. I miss Conie very much. I wish I were with you and Johnny for I could hunt for myself.

*   *   *

My father, Theodore Roosevelt, was the best man I ever knew. He combined strength and courage with gentleness, tenderness, and great unselfishness.[2] He would not tolerate in us children selfishness or cruelty, idleness, cowardice, or untruthfulness. As we grew older he made us understand that the same standard of clean living was demanded for the boys as for the girls; that what was wrong in a woman could not be right in a man. With great love and patience, and the most understanding sympathy and consideration, he combined insistence on discipline. He never physically punished me but once, but he was the only man of whom I was ever really afraid. I do not mean that it was a wrong fear, for he was entirely just, and we children adored him. We used to wait in the library in the evening until we could hear his key rattling. . . and we would troop into his room while he was dressing, to stay there as long as we were permitted, eagerly examining anything which came out of his pockets which could be regarded as an attractive novelty. . . .

I never knew any one who got greater joy out of living than did my father, or any one who more whole-heartedly performed every duty; and no one whom I have ever met approached his combination of enjoyment of life and performance of duty. He and my mother were given to a hospitality that at that time was associated more commonly with Southern than Northern households; and, especially in their later

---

[1] TR to Martha Bulloch Roosevelt, April 28, 1868. In Elting E. Morison and associates, eds., *The Letters of Theodore Roosevelt*, 8 vols. (Cambridge: Harvard University Press, 1951–54), I, 3. Copyright 1951, 1952, 1954, by the President and Fellows of Harvard College. Reprinted by permission of the publisher.

[2] *Theodore Roosevelt: An Autobiography*, Vol. XX of Hermann Hagedorn, ed., *The Works of Theodore Roosevelt*, National Edition, 20 vols. (New York: Charles Scribner's Sons, 1926), 9–11, 13, 15–16, 21. Copyright 1913 by Charles Scribner's Sons; copyright renewed 1941 by Edith K. Carow Roosevelt. Reprinted by permission of the publisher.

years when they had moved up-town in the neighborhood of Central Park, they kept a charming, open house.

My father worked hard at his business, for he died when he was forty-six, too early to have retired. He was interested in every social reform movement, and he did an immense amount of practical charitable work himself. He was a big, powerful man, with a leonine face, and his heart filled with gentleness for those who needed help or protection, and with the possibility of much wrath against a bully or an oppressor. He was very fond of riding both on the road and across country. . . .

My mother, Martha Bulloch, was a sweet, gracious, beautiful Southern woman, a delightful companion and beloved by everybody. She was entirely "unreconstructed" to the day of her death. Her mother, my grandmother, one of the dearest of old ladies, lived with us, and was distinctly overindulgent to us children, being quite unable to harden her heart toward us even when the occasion demanded it. Toward the close of the Civil War, although a very small boy, I grew to have a partial but alert understanding of the fact that the family were not one in their views about that conflict, my father being a strong Lincoln Republican; and once, when I felt that I had been wronged by maternal discipline during the day, I attempted a partial vengeance by praying with loud fervor for the success of the Union arms, when we all came to say our prayers before my mother in the evening. She was not only a most devoted mother, but was also blessed with a strong sense of humor, and she was too much amused to punish me; but I was warned not to repeat the offense, under penalty of my father's being informed—he being the dispenser of serious punishment. . . .

I was a sickly, delicate boy, suffered much from asthma, and frequently had to be taken away on trips to find a place where I could breathe. One of my memories is of my father walking up and down the room with me in his arms at night when I was a very small person, and of sitting up in bed gasping, with my father and mother trying to help me. I went very little to school. I never went to the public schools, as my own children later did, both at the Cove School at Oyster Bay and at the Ford School in Washington. For a few months I attended Professor McMullen's school in Twentieth Street near the house where I was born, but most of the time I had tutors. As I have already said, my aunt taught me when I was small. At one time we had a French governess, a loved and valued "mam'selle," in the household.

When I was ten years old I made my first journey to Europe. My birthday was spent in Cologne, and in order to give me a thoroughly "party" feeling I remember that my mother put on full dress for my birthday dinner. I do not think I gained anything from this particular trip abroad. I cordially hated it, as did my younger brother and sister. Practically all the enjoyment we had was in exploring any ruins or mountains when we could get away from our elders, and in playing in the different hotels. Our one desire was to get back to America, and we regarded Europe with the most ignorant chauvinism and contempt. . . .

When I was fourteen years old, in the winter of '72 and '73, I visited Europe for the second time, and this trip formed a really useful part of my education. We went to Egypt, journeyed up the Nile, travelled through the Holy Land and part of Syria, visited Greece and Constantinople; and then we children spent the summer in a German family in Dresden. My first real collecting as a student of natural history was done in Egypt during this journey.

NATURAL HISTORY

. . . All I can say is that almost as soon as I began to read at all I began to like to read about the natural history of beasts and birds and the more formidable or interesting reptiles and fishes. . . .[3]

I was a very near-sighted small boy, and did not even know that my eyes were not normal until I was fourteen; and so my field studies up to that period were even more worthless than those of the average boy who "collects" natural-history specimens much as he collects stamps. I studied books industriously but nature only so far as could be compassed by a mole-like vision; my triumphs consisted in such things as bringing home and raising—by the aid of milk and a syringe —a family of very young gray squirrels, in fruitlessly endeavoring to tame an excessively unamiable woodchuck, and in making friends with a gentle, pretty, trustful white-footed mouse which reared her family in an empty flower-pot. In order to attract my attention birds had to be as conspicuous as bobolinks or else had to perform feats such as I remember the barn-swallows of my neighborhood once performed, when they assembled for the migration alongside our house and because of some freak of bewilderment swarmed in through the windows and clung helplessly to the curtains, the furniture, and even to our clothes.

Just before my fourteenth birthday my father—then a trustee of the American Museum of Natural History—started me on my rather mothlike career as a naturalist by giving me a pair of spectacles, a French pin-fire double-barrelled shotgun—and lessons in stuffing birds. The spectacles literally opened a new world to me. The mechanism

---

[3] TR, "My Life as a Naturalist," *American Museum Journal,* XVIII (May, 1918), 325–26, 329. Reprinted by permission of *Natural History.*

of the pin-fire gun was without springs and therefore could not get out of order—an important point, as my mechanical ability was nil. The lessons in stuffing and mounting birds were given me by Mr. John G. Bell, a professional taxidermist and collector who had accompanied Audubon on his trip to the then "far West." . . . He taught me as much as my limitations would allow of the art of preparing specimens for scientific use and of mounting them. Some examples of my wooden methods of mounting birds are now in the American Museum: three different species of Egyptian plover, a snowy owl, and a couple of spruce-grouse mounted on a shield with a passenger-pigeon—the three latter killed in Maine during my college vacations.

With my spectacles, my pin-fire gun, and my clumsy industry in skinning "specimens," I passed the winter of '72–'73 in Egypt and Palestine, being then fourteen years old. My collections showed nothing but enthusiasm on my part. I got no bird of any unusual scientific value. My observations were as valueless as my collections save on just one small point; and this point is of interest only as showing, not my own power of observation, but the ability of good men to fail to observe or record the seemingly self-evident. . . .

. . . I never grew to have keen powers of observation. But whatever I did see I saw truly, and I was fairly apt to understand what it meant. In other words, I saw what was sufficiently obvious, and in such case did not usually misinterpret what I had seen. . . .

After returning to this country and until I was half-way through college, I continued to observe and collect in the fashion of the ordinary boy who is interested in natural history. I made copious and valueless notes. As I said above, I did not see and observe very keenly; later it interested and rather chagrined me to find out how much more C. Hart Merriam and John Burroughs saw when I went out with them near Washington or in the Yellowstone Park. . . .

While in Harvard I was among those who joined in forming the Nuttall Club, which I believe afterward became one of the parent sources of the American Ornithologists' Union.

The Harvard of that day was passing through a phase of biological study which was shaped by the belief that German university methods were the only ones worthy of copy, and also by the proper admiration for the younger Agassiz, whose interest was mainly in the lower forms of marine life. . . .

But I never lost a real interest in natural history; and I very keenly regret that at certain times I did not display this interest in more practical fashion.

2
Politics and Reform

*Theodore Roosevelt could not resist the lure of poli-
tics; he became a professional politician. The selections that
follow illuminate his basic convictions, his administrative talent,
his desire for power. They reveal his early reformism, his independence, and his dissatisfaction with the prevailing politics of the
Gilded Age. But these writings also disclose his party regularity,
his distrust of the Mugwumps, and his struggle to come to terms
with the Republican hierarchy without sacrificing his integrity
and independence. This was not easy to do, but on the whole the
young New Yorker was successful. By 1900, as John M. Blum has
written, he had "effected a synthesis of experience which allowed
him to act as well as to believe."*

IN THE LEGISLATURE

. . . The men I knew best were the men in the clubs of social
pretension and the men of cultivated taste and easy life.[1] When I
began to make inquiries as to the whereabouts of the local Republican
association and the means of joining it, these men—and the big business men and lawyers also—laughed at me, and told me that politics
were "low"; that the organizations were not controlled by "gentlemen"; that, I would find them run by saloon-keepers, horse-car con-
ductors, and the like, and not by men with any of whom I would come
in contact outside; and, moreover, they assured me that the men I
met would be rough and brutal and unpleasant to deal with. I
answered that if this were so it merely meant that the people I knew
did not belong to the governing class, and that the other people did—
and that I intended to be one of the governing class; that if they
proved too hard-bit for me I supposed I would have to quit, but that
I certainly would not quit until I had made the effort and found
out whether I really was too weak to hold my own in the rough and
tumble. . . .

[1] *Theodore Roosevelt: An Autobiography,* Vol. XX of Hermann Hagedorn,
ed., *The Works of Theodore Roosevelt,* National Edition, 20 vols. (New York:
Charles Scribner's Sons, 1926), 59, 66. Coypright 1913 by Charles Scribner's Sons;
copyright renewed 1941 by Edith K. Carow Roosevelt. Reprinted by permission
of the publisher.

I was elected to the legislature in the fall of 1881, and found myself the youngest man in that body. I was re-elected the two following years. Like all young men and inexperienced members, I had considerable difficulty in teaching myself to speak. I profited much by the advice of a hard-headed old countryman—who was unconsciously paraphrasing the Duke of Wellington, who was himself doubtless paraphrasing somebody else. The advice ran: "Don't speak until you are sure you have something to say, and know just what it is; then say it, and sit down."

My first days in the legislature were much like those of a boy in a strange school. My fellow legislators and I eyed one another with mutual distrust. Each of us chose his seat, each began by following the lead of some veteran in the first routine matters, and then, in a week or two, we began to drift into groups according to our several affinities. The legislature was Democratic. I was a Republican from the "silk-stocking" district, the wealthiest district in New York, and I was put as one of the minority members, on the Committee of Cities.

*   *   *

Mr. Speaker,[2] . . . The men who were mainly concerned in this fraud are known throughout New York as men whose financial dishonesty is a matter of common notoriety. I make that statement deliberately; that the three or four wealthy stock gamblers who are interested in those roads are men who would be barely trusted in financial operations by any reputable business man . . . .

Judge Westbrook's share in the transaction did not come in until about June 13, when the suit was brought before him. He then expressed in his opinion strongly and emphatically that it [the Manhattan Elevated Railway Company] was a swindle from the beginning. . . .

The affair went on, and on the 21st of October last, the Judge declared, in a speech, that the corporation was a swindle—declared it emphatically without any reserve. Four days later he does not write, but telegraphs down an order allowing the road to go out of the hands of the receivers back into the hands of the Manhattan Company, which by that time has become synonymous with getting into the hands of Jay Gould, Cyrus W. Field and Russell Sage. That was four days after he said it was a swindle. He puts the whole road in the hands of the swindlers. . . .

[2] New York Times, April 7, 1882. Roosevelt was discussing the so-called Westbrook case. At the beginning of the legislative session of 1882, the young assemblyman created a sensation by demanding that the assembly investigate reports that Judge Theodore R. Westbrook of the State Supreme Court had conspired with Jay Gould and other prominent businessmen in a "stock-jobbing" scheme to gain control of the Manhattan Elevated Railway. Roosevelt managed to secure the adoption of a resolution for an inquiry, but the committee making the investigation eventually exonerated Judge Westbrook. The affair was important in Roosevelt's early career, for it stamped him as something of a crusader and brought him his first public acclaim.

We have a right to demand that our judiciary should be kept beyond reproach; and we have a right to demand that if we find men against whom there is not only suspicion, but almost a certainty that they have had collusion with men whose interests were in conflict with the interests of the public, they shall, at least, be required to bring positive facts with which to prove there has not been such collusion. . . .

I am aware that it ought to have been done by a man of more experience and, possibly, an abler source than myself, but as nobody else chose to demand it, I certainly would in the interest of the Commonwealth of New York. . . . This is a most important investigation and it should be treated with due weight, and I hope my resolution will prevail.

*   *   *

In the legislature the problems with which I dealt were mainly problems of honesty and decency and of legislative and administrative efficiency.[3] They represented the effort, the wise, the vitally necessary effort, to get efficient and honest government. But as yet I understood little of the effort which was already beginning, for the most part under very bad leadership, to secure a more genuine social and industrial justice. . . .

I did, however, have one exceedingly useful experience. A bill was introduced by the Cigarmakers' Union to prohibit the manufacture of cigars in tenement-houses. I was appointed one of a committee of three to investigate conditions in the tenement-houses and see if legislation should be had. . . . As a matter of fact, I had supposed I would be against the legislation, and I rather think that I was put on the committee with that idea, for the respectable people I knew were against it; it was contrary to the principles of political economy of the *laissez-faire* kind; and business men who spoke to me about it shook their heads and said that it was designed to prevent a man doing as he wished and as he had a right to do with what was his own.

However, my first visits to the tenement-house districts in question made me feel that, whatever the theories might be, as a matter of practical common sense I could not conscientiously vote for the continuance of the conditions which I saw. These conditions rendered it impossible for the families of the tenement-house workers to live so that the children might grow up fitted for the exacting duties of American citizenship. I visited the tenement-houses once with my colleagues of the committee, once with some of the labor-union representatives, and once or twice by myself. In a few of the tenement-houses there were suites of rooms ample in number where the work on the tobacco was done in rooms not occupied for cooking or sleeping or living. In the overwhelming majority of cases, however, there were one, two, or

---

[3] *The Works of Theodore Roosevelt*, XX, 81–84. Reprinted by permission of Charles Scribner's Sons.

three room apartments, and the work of manufacturing the tobacco by men, women, and children went on day and night in the eating, living, and sleeping rooms—sometimes in one room. I have always remembered one room in which two families were living. On my inquiry as to who the third adult male was I was told that he was a boarder with one of the families. There were several children, three men, and two women in this room. The tobacco was stowed about everywhere, alongside the foul bedding, and in a corner where there were scraps of food. The men, women, and children in this room worked by day and far on into the evening, and they slept and ate there. They were Bohemians, unable to speak English, except that one of the children knew enough to act as interpreter.

Instead of opposing the bill I ardently championed it. It was a poorly drawn measure, and the governor, Grover Cleveland, was at first doubtful about signing it. The Cigarmakers' Union then asked me to appear before the governor and argue for it. I accordingly did so, acting as spokesman for the battered, undersized foreigners who represented the Union and the workers. The governor signed the bill. Afterward this tenement-house cigar legislation was declared invalid by the court of appeals in the Jacobs decision. . . . It was this case which first waked me to a dim and partial understanding of the fact that the courts were not necessarily the best judges of what should be done to better social and industrial conditions.

THE CAMPAIGN OF 1884

. . . I intend to vote the Republican presidential ticket.[4] While at Chicago, I told Mr. Lodge that such was my intention; but, before announcing it, I wished to have time to think the whole matter over. A man cannot act both without and within the party; he can do either, but he cannot possibly do both. Each course has its advantages, and each has its disadvantages, and one cannot take the advantages or the disadvantages separately. I went in with my eyes open to do what I could within the party; I did my best and got beaten; and I propose to stand by the result. It is impossible to combine the functions of a guerilla chief with those of a colonel in the regular army; one has greater independence of action, the other is able to make what action he does take vastly more effective. In certain contingencies the one can do most good, in certain contingencies the other; but there is no use in accepting a commission and then trying to play the game out on a lone hand. During the entire canvass for the nomination, Mr. Blaine received but two checks—one was at the Utica convention, the

[4] Interview in the Boston *Herald*, July 20, 1884.

other was the Powell Clayton incident. I had a hand in both, and I could have had a hand in neither had not those Republicans who at Utica elected me as the head of the New York State delegation supposed that I would in good faith support the man who was fairly made the Republican nominee.

I am by inheritance and by education a Republican; whatever good I have been able to accomplish in public life has been accomplished through the Republican party; I have acted with it in the past, and wish to act with it in the future; I went as a regular delegate to the Chicago convention, and I intend to abide by the outcome of that convention. I am going back in a day or two to my Western ranches, as I do not expect to take any part in the campaign this fall.

THE SPOILS SYSTEM AND CIVIL SERVICE REFORM

. . . The purpose of the Civil Service Commission is to secure an absolutely nonpartisan public service; to have men appointed to and retained in office wholly without reference to their politics.[5] In other words, we desire to make a man's honesty and capacity to do the work to which he is assigned the sole tests of his appointment and retention. In the departmental service at Washington we have succeeded in putting a nearly complete stop to removals for political purposes. Men are retained in the departments almost wholly without regard to politics. But it has been a matter of more difficulty to get them to come forward and enter the examinations without regard to politics.

The task set us is very difficult. We have to face the intense and interested hostility of the great mass of self-seeking politicians, and of the much larger mass of office-seekers, whose only hope of acquiring office rests in political influence, and is immediately cut off by the application of any, even the most modest, merit test. We have to overcome popular indifference or ignorance, and we have to do constant battle with that spirit of mean and vicious cynicism which so many men, respectable enough in their private life, assume as their attitude in public affairs.

Our chief difficulty, however, arises from the slowness with which the popular mind takes to any new theory, and from its inability, by no means wholly unnatural, to discriminate between the branches of the service where the law does apply and those where it does not. For over sixty years American citizens have grown accustomed to seeing the public service treated as so much plunder, to be parceled out among the adherents of the victorious party for the time being. No

[5] TR, "An Object Lesson in Civil Service Reform," *Atlantic Monthly*, LXVII (February, 1891), 252.

other cause during these sixty years has been so potent in effecting the degradation of public life and in working a real and serious harm to the national character. In the course of the last few years a portion of the public service, that known as the classified service, with which alone the Commission has to do, has been withdrawn from the degrading and demoralizing effects of this patronage system; but the greater portion still remains outside the classified service, and therefore in the hands of the spoilsmongers.

* * *

I am informed by the local board of examiners of the Baltimore Post-Office that at present few but Republicans apply to be examined for the positions of carriers and clerks in that office.[6] In view of the approaching August examinations I wish to make through your columns a statement to all Democrats, and to all citizens generally, without regard to party affiliations, who may think of applying for such positions. On behalf of the Civil Service Commission I desire to extend an earnest invitation to all who wish to enter the classified service at the Baltimore Post-Office to come forward and be examined. The commission will do all in its power to see that they are treated with perfect fairness, irrespective of their party affiliations, and will guarantee that their papers will be marked and their names listed and certified for appointment exactly according to the averages they make for themselves in the examination.

It is illegal for the postmaster or any appointing officer to refuse to appoint, or to discriminate in any way against, any candidate for a place in the classified service because of his politics. The law is designed expressly to secure an equal chance to Republicans and Democrats. Democrats have exactly the same right that Republicans have to examination and certification by the commission and to appointment by the postmaster or other appointing officer. Under the law affecting the classified service it is an offense, punishable by removal from office, for the postmaster or any similar officer to try to find out a man's politics, or to take politics into account in any way in making appointments.

I sincerely hope that every young man, whatever his politics, Democratic or otherwise, who desires to enter the government service as a clerk or carrier in the Baltimore Post-Office will come forward at the next examination. We guarantee him fair play as far as we are concerned. It is our especial desire to get Democrats to enter these examinations as freely as Republicans, and we shall do all in our power to see that political considerations are given no weight in making ap-

*TR to the Editor of the Baltimore *Sun,* June, 1890. Reprinted in *Civil Service Reformer,* VI (July, 1890), 73.

pointments, and that all applicants, Democrats and Republicans, are treated alike.

THE NEW YORK POLICE BOARD

We have called you here to tell you what we expect and have a right to expect of you.[7] Some of those whose places you took we reduced because of inefficiency. We found in two precincts that the roundsmen made few or no complaints on the last tour. They said it was because the discipline of the squads was so good that there was none to make. We sent our new roundsmen into the precincts and we found out that only in one precinct was that true. There we left all the roundsmen untouched. In the other it was not true. Our men made six complaints one night and five the next. Then we removed all the squad men.

We shall judge you largely by the discipline of the force under you. I am disappointed in the way the men patrol yet after all we have said. They don't patrol; they lounge and gossip. Five minutes is ample time for a policeman to talk over any business he has with any one on his post. We expect you to keep your men moving.

We don't want a flood of petty complaints. We shall not judge you by the number of complaints you make, but by the way you keep your men up to their duty.

Some of you owe your promotion to individual acts of bravery. There is one whose promotion we with great regret had to refuse to make permanent. He had shown great gallantry, but we were compelled to admit that he was not doing his duty as he should.

In other cases we have allowed the proved courage of the man to guide us. But we know that the quality of daring does not always gauge a man's common sense and discretion. It devolves upon you to show that we have made no mistake.

Each of you knows that he owes his promotion to nothing but his own record of merit. No friend spoke for you; no friend can help you and no enemy harm you, as long as you do your duty. One of you who deserved promotion we hesitated about long because a friend kept writing asking for it. We don't like that and we don't want it; take that to heart. And it is not needed.

We want of you first—honesty. We have reduced some men because we could not feel sure they were absolutely honest. We will turn any man out the moment we find that out about him. Next we demand of

[7] Remarks addressed to twenty-two newly promoted roundsmen, November 30, 1895. In New York *Sun,* November 30, 1895.

you courage. Every one of you has got to be as ready to risk life and limb, if need be, as if he wore the uniform of the national army. Cowardice we will never pardon. The board has full confidence in you. Lastly, we want of you vigilance, energy, and common sense. No staying in the station-house on the last tour. Don't be heaping up little complaints about men being off their relieving points. You are to see that the saloons are closed on Sunday, and you are to see to it just as well that burglars and thieves are kept out of your precincts. If we find many burglaries in one, we shall put not only the patrolmen on trial on whose post they are, but the roundsmen as well, whose duty it is to keep them vigilant.

I don't know the politics of one of you. I care as little for your politics as about your religion. What the board cares for is that you shall be a credit to the force. You have won your promotion on your merits. You will keep it as long as you deserve it. If any one of you proves his title to go up higher, up he will go, be sure of it. We expect you to justify our choice of you all.

*　　*　　*

My Dear Mr. Mayor:[8] I herewith tender you my resignation, to take effect on April 19, in accordance with our understanding.

I wish to take this opportunity, sir, to thank you for appointing me and to express my very deep appreciation of your attitude toward me and toward the force, the direction of which you in part entrusted to my care. . . . In this Department we, as well as you, have been hampered by unwise legislation. . . .

Nevertheless, very much has been accomplished. For the first time the police force has been administered without regard to politics and with an honest and resolute purpose to enforce the laws equitably and to show favor to no man. The old system of blackmail and corruption has been almost entirely broken up; we have greatly improved the standard of discipline; we have preserved complete order, and we have warred against crime and vice more effectively than ever before. The fact that we have come short in any measure is due simply to the folly of the law which deprives us of the full measure of power over our subordinates, which could alone guarantee the best results. We have administered the Civil Service law in spirit and in letter so as to show that there is not the slightest excuse for wishing to get rid of it, or for claiming that it does not produce the best possible results when honestly enforced. . . .

. . . In promotions and appointments alike we have disregarded wholly all considerations of political or religious creed; we have treated

[8] TR to Mayor William L. Strong, April 17, 1897. In New York *Sun,* April 17, 1897.

all men alike on their merits, rewarding the good and punishing the bad without reference to outside considerations. . . .

During my term of service we have striven especially to make the police force not only the terror of the burglar, the rioter, the tough, the law-breaker and criminal of every kind, but also the ready ally of every movement for good. One of my pleasantest experiences has been working with all men, rich and poor, priests and laymen, Catholics and Protestants, Jews and Gentiles, who are striving to make our civic conditions better, who are striving to raise the standard of living, of morality and of comfort among our less fortunate brethren. We have endeavored to make all men and all societies engaged in such work feel that the police were their natural allies. We have endeavored to make the average private citizen feel that the officer of the law was to be dreaded only by the law-breaker and was ever ready to treat with courtesy and to befriend any one who needed his aid.

The man in the ranks, the man with the night stick, has been quick to respond to all efforts, quick to recognize honesty of purpose in his superiors. You have in the police force a body of admirable men, brave, able and zealous; under proper leadership they can at any time be depended upon to do the best possible work.

THE CAMPAIGN OF 1896

. . . The Populists really represent very little except an angry but loose discontent with affairs as they actually are, and a readiness to grasp after any remedy proposed either by charlatanism or by an ignorance as honest as it is abysmal.[9] The Populist party, therefore, waxes and wanes inversely as prosperity increases or declines; that is, the folly of certain voters seems to grow in inverse ratio to their need of displaying wisdom. At present, affairs over the country seem to be on the mend, and the Populist party is therefore losing power. The Democratic attitude toward free silver, in turn, depends very much upon the Populists' strength. Wherever and whenever the Populists are a distinct menace to the government, the Democrats try to outbid them by declaring in favor of unsound finance; but as the Populists become weak, the mass of the Democratic statesmen grow ready once more to stand by their party, even should that party decline to announce itself as unrestrictedly as they wish in favor of dishonest money. . . .

The Republican party's attitude, on the contrary, is absolutely clear. It does not depend in the least upon whether the crops are good or bad, upon whether the business community is or is not in a flourishing

---

[9] TR, "The Issues of 1896," *Century Magazine*, LI (November, 1895), 69–70, 72.

condition. It does not even depend upon who is nominated. From Iowa east every Republican State has declared, or will declare, in some shape, against the adoption of a free-silver platform; and even west of Iowa the majority of Republicans, in all save the few rabid silver States, are against free silver and in favor of sound finance. Every Republican whose nomination is a possibility is against the free coinage of silver, and has proved his faith by his votes and actions in time past. . . .

The Republican party will go into the next election as the champion of the only foreign policy to which self-respecting Americans can subscribe; and the Democratic party, on this issue, will either have to condemn without reservation its own immediate past, or else must stand as the apologist of a policy of national humiliation.

More important, almost, than any specific measure or policy is the general attitude of the Republican party toward good government. A party is much more than its candidate or its platform. It is even more than the men who, in the aggregate, compose it at the moment; for it is a bundle of traditions, tendencies, and principles as well. Every act of an organized Republican body in any portion of the Union has some effect upon the general party welfare. Republicans, and specially Republican politicians, in and out of office, must, if they have the welfare of the party at heart, feel that a heavy responsibility rests upon them. They must take the right side on every issue that arises, local or State or National. It is a discredit to the whole party when Republicans put into office a scoundrel of any kind. It is a credit to the whole party when they work in any place disinterestedly for good government. They must feel this, and they must show that they feel it. Everywhere they must stand for law and order. The law-breaker, whether he be lyncher or whitecapper, or merely the liquor-seller who desires to drive an illegal business, must be made to feel that the Republican party is against him. Every ballot-box stuffer, every bribe-taking legislator, every corrupt official of any grade, must be made to feel that he is an outcast from the Republican party. The party must stand firmly for good government in our cities; and in many cases this good government can only be obtained by the sinking of partisan lines in municipal contests. The Republican party must stand by the civil-service law, National and State. Republicans of every grade must feel that it behooves them to see that their party representatives in every office are clean and honest men; and for the sake of the welfare of the party they must rigorously punish the scoundrels who use the party name to cloak their own base purposes. On the great national issues of the day —the tariff, finance, and foreign policy—the Republican party has all the advantage of position in the presidential fight upon which we shall shortly enter.

GOVERNOR OF NEW YORK

. . . My great object as Governor was to do reform work—not merely talk about it, but do it.[10] I put through the best Civil Service Reform law that is to be found anywhere on the statute books whether of the nation or of any of the States. I made the first great advance in the proper taxation of special franchises enjoyed by enormously wealthy individuals and corporations. Above all, I literally revolutionized the public service by the character of the men whom I appointed. When I ended my term the State service of New York was conducted on as high a level of integrity and capacity as any first-class business undertaking. I doubt if there was a state in the world, English-speaking or otherwise, where the standard was higher in either respect.

[10] TR to Philip Henry Goepp, March 18, 1901. In Elting E. Morison and associates, eds., *The Letters of Theodore Roosevelt*, 8 vols. (Cambridge: Harvard University Press, 1951–54), III, 18. Copyright 1951, 1952, 1954, by the President and Fellows of Harvard College. Reprinted by permission of the publisher.

3

The Strenuous Life

Roosevelt was extraordinarily broad in the range of his interests, but he was absorbed throughout life in what Henry F. Pringle has called "the Gospel of Strenuosity." Roosevelt's youthful determination to develop his puny body, his interest in nature, his ranching and hunting experiences, and the compulsive vitality of his later years all attested to his passionate concern for physical vigor and achievement. It was appropriate that a collection of his essays published in 1900 should be entitled The Strenuous Life. *His definition of the "strenuous life" was broad and far-ranging in its implications, constituting, in fact, an essential part of his basic beliefs and attitudes—a philosophy "of bodily vigor as a method of getting that vigor of soul without which vigor of the body counts for nothing." The documents in this section describe a few of TR's experiences and reveal his strong opinions about the desirability of competitive athletics, physical fitness, and an active life. They also suggest the overcompensation evident in his lifelong philosophy of the strenuous life.*

HUNTING

It was late in the afternoon before we saw any game; then we made out in the middle of a large plain three black specks, which proved to be buffalo—old bulls.[1] Our horses had come a good distance, under a hot sun, and, as they had had no water except from the mud-hole in the morning, they were in no condition for running. They were not very fast, anyhow; so, though the ground was unfavorable, we made up our minds to try to creep up to the buffalo. We left the ponies in a hollow half a mile from the game, and started off on our hands and knees, taking advantage of every sage-brush as cover. After a while we had to lie flat on our bodies and wriggle like snakes; and while doing this I blundered into a bed of cactus, and filled my hands

[1] Hermann Hagedorn, ed., *The Works of Theodore Roosevelt,* National Edition, 20 vols. (New York: Charles Scribner's Sons, 1926), I, 200, 205–6. Copyright 1926 by Charles Scribner's Sons. Reprinted by permission of the publisher.

with the spines. After taking advantage of every hollow, hillock, or sage-brush, we got within about a hundred and twenty-five or fifty yards of where the three bulls were unconsciously feeding, and as all between was bare ground I drew up and fired. It was the first time I ever shot at buffalo, and, confused by the bulk and shaggy hair of the beast, I aimed too far back at one that was standing nearly broadside on toward me. The bullet told on his body with a loud crack, the dust flying up from his hide; but it did not work him any immediate harm, or in the least hinder him from making off; and away went all three, with their tails up, disappearing over a light rise in the ground.

Much disgusted, we trotted back to where the horses were picketed, jumped on them, a good deal out of breath, and rode after the flying game. . . .

So far the trip had certainly not been a success, although sufficiently varied as regards its incidents. We had been confined to moist biscuits for three days as our food; had been wet and cold at night, and sunburned until our faces peeled in the day; were hungry and tired, and had met with bad weather and all kinds of accidents; in addition to which I had shot badly. . . .

Shortly after midday we left the creek bottom, and skirted a ridge of broken buttes, cut up by the gullies and winding ravines, in whose bottoms grew bunch-grass. While passing near the mouth and to leeward of one of these ravines both ponies threw up their heads and snuffed the air, turning their muzzles toward the head of the gully. Feeling sure that they had smelt some wild beast, either a bear or a buffalo, I slipped off my pony and ran quickly but cautiously up along the valley. Before I had gone a hundred yards, I noticed in the soft soil at the bottom the round prints of a bison's hoofs; and immediately afterward got a glimpse of the animal himself, as he fed slowly up the course of the ravine, some distance ahead of me. The wind was just right, and no ground could have been better for stalking. Hardly needing to bend down, I walked up behind a small sharp-crested hillock and, peeping over, there below me, not fifty yards off, was a great bison bull. He was walking along, grazing as he walked. His glossy fall coat was in fine trim and shone in the rays of the sun, while his pride of bearing showed him to be in the lusty vigor of his prime. As I rose above the crest of the hill, he held up his head and cocked his tail to the air. Before he could go off, I put the bullet in behind his shoulder. The wound was an almost immediately fatal one, yet with surprising agility for so large and heavy an animal, he bounded up the opposite side of the ravine, heedless of two more balls, both of which went into his flank and ranged forward, and disappeared over the ridge at a lumbering gallop, the blood pouring from his mouth and nostrils. We knew he could not go far, and trotted leisurely along on his bloody trail; and in the next gully we found him stark dead, lying almost on his back, having pitched over the side when he tried to go down it. His head was a remarkably fine one, even for a fall buffalo.

* * *

At last, as I was thinking of turning toward camp, I stole up to the crest of one of the ridges, and looked over into the valley some sixty yards off.[2] Immediately I caught the loom of some large, dark object; and another glance showed me a big grizzly walking slowly off with his head down. He was quartering to me, and I fired into his flank, the bullet, as I afterward found, ranging forward and piercing one lung. At the shot he uttered a loud, moaning grunt, and plunged forward at a heavy gallop, while I raced obliquely down the hill to cut him off. After going a few hundred feet he reached a laurel thicket, some thirty yards broad, and two or three times as long, which he did not leave. I ran up to the edge and there halted, not liking to venture into the mass of twisted, close-growing stems and glossy foliage. Moreover, as I halted, I heard him utter a peculiar, savage kind of whine from the heart of the brush. Accordingly, I began to skirt the edge, standing on tiptoe and gazing earnestly to see if I could not catch a glimpse of his hide. When I was at the narrowest part of the thicket, he suddenly left it directly opposite, and then wheeled and stood broadside to me on the hillside, a little above. He turned his head stiffly toward me; scarlet strings of froth hung from his lips; his eyes burned like embers in the gloom.

I held true, aiming behind the shoulder, and my bullet shattered the point or lower end of his heart, taking out a big nick. Instantly the great bear turned with a harsh roar of fury and challenge, blowing the bloody foam from his mouth, so that I saw the gleam of his white fangs; and then he charged straight at me, crashing and bounding through the laurel bushes, so that it was hard to aim. I waited till he came to a fallen tree, raking him as he topped it with a ball, which entered his chest and went through the cavity of his body, but he neither swerved nor flinched, and at the moment I did not know that I had struck him. He came steadily on, and in another second was almost upon me. I fired for his forehead, but my bullet went low, entering his open mouth, smashing his lower jaw and going into the neck. I leaped to one side almost as I pulled the trigger; and through the hanging smoke the first thing I saw was his paw as he made a vicious side blow at me. The rush of his charge carried him past. As he struck he lurched forward, leaving a pool of bright blood where his muzzle hit the ground; but he recovered himself and made two or three jumps onward, while I hurriedly jammed a couple of cartridges into the magazine, my rifle holding only four, all of which I had fired. Then he

[2] Hagedorn, ed., *The Works of Theodore Roosevelt*, II, 240–42. Reprinted by permission of the publisher.

tried to pull up, but as he did so his muscles seemed suddenly to give way, his head drooped, and he rolled over and over like a shot rabbit. Each of my first three bullets had inflicted a mortal wound.

. . . The beauty of the trophy, and the memory of the circumstances under which I procured it, make me value it perhaps more highly than any other in my house.

THE WILD WEST

Though I had previously made a trip into the then Territory of Dakota, beyond the Red River, it was not until 1883 that I went to the Little Missouri, and there took hold of two cattle-ranches, the Chimney Butte and the Elkhorn.[3]

It was still the Wild West in those days, the far West, the West of Owen Wister's stories and Frederic Remington's drawings, the West of the Indian and the buffalo-hunter, the soldier and the cow-puncher. That land of the West has gone now, "gone, gone with lost Atlantis," gone to the isle of ghosts and of strange dead memories. It was a land of vast silent spaces, of lonely rivers, and of plains where the wild game stared at the passing horseman. It was a land of scattered ranches, of herds of long-horned cattle, and of reckless riders who unmoved looked in the eyes of life or of death. In that land we led a free and hardy life, with horse and with rifle. We worked under the scorching midsummer sun, when the wide plains shimmered and wavered in the heat; and we knew the freezing misery of riding night guard round the cattle in the late fall round-up. In the soft springtime the stars were glorious in our eyes each night before we fell asleep; and in the winter we rode through blinding blizzards, when the driven snow-dust burned our faces. There were monotonous days, as we guided the trail cattle or the beef herds, hour after hour, at the slowest of walks; and minutes or hours teeming with excitement as we stopped stampedes or swam the herds across rivers treacherous with quicksands or brimmed with running ice. We knew toil and hardship and hunger and thirst; and we saw men die violent deaths as they worked among the horses and cattle, or fought in evil feuds with one another; but we felt the beat of hardy life in our veins, and ours was the glory of work and the joy of living.

*   *   *

Meanwhile I took the three thieves into Dickinson, the nearest town.[4] The going was bad, and the little mares could only drag the

---

[3] Hagedorn, ed., *The Works of Theodore Roosevelt*, XX, 96–97. Reprinted by permission of the publisher.

[4] Hagedorn, ed., *The Works of Theodore Roosevelt*, I, 397–98. Reprinted by permission of the publisher.

wagon at a walk; so, though we drove during the daylight, it took us two days and a night to make the journey. It was a most desolate drive. The prairie had been burned the fall before, and was a mere bleak waste of blackened earth, and a cold, rainy mist lasted throughout the two days. The only variety was where the road crossed the shallow headwaters of Knife and Green Rivers. Here the ice was high along the banks, and the wagon had to be taken to pieces to get it over. My three captives were unarmed, but as I was alone with them, except for the driver, of whom I knew nothing, I had to be doubly on my guard, and never let them come close to me. The little mares went so slowly, and the heavy road rendered any hope of escape by flogging up the horses so entirely out of the question, that I soon found the safest plan was to put the prisoners in the wagon and myself walk behind with the inevitable Winchester. Accordingly I trudged steadily the whole time behind the wagon through the ankle-deep mud. It was a gloomy walk. Hour after hour went by always the same, while I plodded along through the dreary landscape—hunger, cold, and fatigue struggling with a sense of dogged, weary resolution. At night, when we put up at the squalid hut of a frontier granger, the only habitation on our road, it was even worse. I did not dare to go to sleep, but making my three men get into the upper bunk, from which they could get out only with difficulty, I sat up with my back against the cabin door and kept watch over them all night long. So, after thirty-six hours' sleeplessness, I was most heartily glad when we at last jolted into the long, straggling main street of Dickinson, and I was able to give my unwilling companions into the hands of the sheriff.

THE ATHLETIC SPIRIT

One reason why I so thoroughly believe in the athletic spirit at Harvard is because the athletic spirit is essentially democratic.[5] Our chief interest should not lie in the great champions in sport. On the contrary, our concern should be most of all to widen the base, the foundation in athletic sports, to encourage in every way a healthy rivalry which shall give to the largest possible number of students the chance to take part in vigorous outdoor games. It is of far more importance that a man shall play something himself, even if he plays it badly, than that he shall go with hundreds of companions to see some one else play well, and it is not healthy for either students or athletes if the terms are mutually exclusive. . . .

As I emphatically disbelieve in seeing Harvard or any other college

[5] From an address at the Harvard Union, Harvard University, February 23, 1907. In Willis Fletcher Johnson, ed., *Addresses and Papers of Theodore Roosevelt* (New York, 1909), pp. 348–50.

turn out mollycoddles instead of vigorous men, I may add that I do not in the least object to a sport because it is rough. Rowing, baseball, lacrosse, track and field games, hockey, football are all of them good. Moreover, it is to my mind simple nonsense, a mere confession of weakness, to desire to abolish a game because tendencies show themselves, or practices grow up, which prove that the game ought to be reformed. . . .

We cannot afford to turn out of college men who shrink from physical effort or from a little physical pain. In any republic courage is a prime necessity for the average citizen if he is to be a good citizen, and he needs physical courage no less than moral courage, the courage that dares as well as the courage that endures, the courage that will fight valiantly alike against the foes of the soul and the foes of the body. Athletics are good, especially in their rougher forms, because they tend to develop such courage. They are good also because they encourage a true democratic spirit, for in the athletic field the man must be judged not with reference to outside and accidental attributes, but to that combination of bodily vigor and moral quality which go to make up prowess.

I trust I need not add that in defending athletics I would not for one moment be understood as excusing that perversion of athletics which would make it the end of life instead of merely a means in life. It is first-class healthful play, and is useful as such. But play is not business, and it is a very poor business indeed for a college man to learn nothing but sport.

THE LIFE OF STRENUOUS ENDEAVOR

. . . I wish to preach, not the doctrine of ignoble ease, but the doctrine of the strenuous life; the life of toil and effort; of labor and strife; to preach that highest form of success which comes, not to the man who desires more easy peace, but to the man who does not shrink from danger, from hardship or from bitter toil, and who out of these wins the splendid ultimate triumph.[6]

A life of ignoble ease, a life of that peace which springs merely from lack either of desire or of power to strive after great things, is as little worthy of a nation as of an individual. I ask only that what every self-respecting American demands from himself, and from his sons, shall be demanded of the American nation as a whole. Who among you would teach your boys that ease, that peace is to be the first consideration in their eyes,—to be the ultimate goal after which they strive. . . .

[6] From an address to the Hamilton Club of Chicago, April 10, 1899. In State of New York, *Public Papers of Theodore Roosevelt, Governor, 1899* (Albany, 1899), pp. 293–95, 297, 306–7.

As it is with the individual so it is with the nation. It is a base untruth to say that happy is the nation that has no history. Thrice happy is the nation that has a glorious history. Far better it is to dare mighty things, to win glorious triumphs, even though checkered by failure, than to take rank with those poor spirits who neither enjoy much nor suffer much, because they live in the gray twilight that knows neither victory nor defeat. . . .

. . . The timid man, the lazy man, the man who distrusts his country, the over-civilized man who has lost the great fighting, masterful virtues, the ignorant man and the man of dull mind, whose soul is incapable of feeling the mighty lift that thrills "Stern men with empires in their brains"—all these of course shrink from seeing the nation undertake its new duties; shrink from seeing us build a navy and army adequate to our needs; shrink from seeing us do our share of the world's work, by bringing order out of chaos in the great, fair tropic islands from which the valor of our soldiers and sailors has driven the Spanish flag. These are the men who fear the strenuous life, who fear the only national life which is really worth leading. They believe in that cloistered life which saps the hardy virtues in a nation, as it saps them in the individual; or else they are wedded to that base spirit of gain and greed which recognizes in commercialism the be-all and end-all of national life, instead of realizing that, though an indispensable element, it is after all but one of the many elements that go to make up true national greatness. . . .

. . . The twentieth century looms before us big with the fate of many nations. . . . Let us therefore boldly face the life of strife, resolute to do our duty well and manfully; resolute to uphold righteousness by deed and by word; resolute to be both honest and brave, to serve high ideals, yet to use practical methods. Above all, let us not shrink from strife, moral or physical, within or without the nation, provided we are certain that the strife is justified; for it is only through strife, through hard and dangerous endeavor, that we shall ultimately win the goal of true national greatness.

4
The Good Citizen

Nothing was more integral to Theodore Roosevelt's personal philosophy than his belief in the value of hard work and his faith in the importance of individual character. He preached, from early manhood until the day he died, the high ideals and responsibilities of citizenship. The hortatory and platitudinous nature of this ceaseless sermonizing should not blind us to its influence in shaping TR's politics and in determining the images he evoked in the minds of his contemporaries. It was his passionate affirmation of the need for the good citizen along with his celebration of duty and devotion to cause that made him such a famous spokesman for civic righteousness and such a vivid symbol of practical idealism in his day. In the items reprinted below Roosevelt defines the good citizen and discloses some of his hopes and fears about American society.

PATRIOTISM

I am peculiarly glad to have an opportunity of addressing you, my fellow citizens of Dakota, on the Fourth of July, because it always seems to me that those who dwell in a new territory, and whose actions, therefore, are peculiarly fruitful, for good and for bad alike, in shaping the future, have in consequence peculiar responsibilities.[1] You have already been told, very truthfully and effectively, of the great gifts and blessings you enjoy; and we all of us feel, most rightly and properly, that we belong to the greatest nation that has ever existed on this earth—a feeling I like to see, for I wish every American always to keep the most intense pride in his country, and people. But as you already know your rights and privileges so well, I am going to ask you to excuse me if I say a few words to you about your duties. . . .

We have rights, but we have correlative duties; none can escape them. We only have the right to live on as free men, governing our

[1] From an address delivered in the Dakota Territory, July 4, 1886. In Hermann Hagedorn, *Roosevelt in the Bad Lands* (Boston: Houghton Mifflin Company, 1921), pp. 407–10. Copyright 1921 by Houghton Mifflin Company. Reprinted by permission of the publisher.

own lives as we will, so long as we show ourselves worthy of the privileges we enjoy. We must remember that the Republic can only be kept pure by the individual purity of its members; and that if it become once thoroughly corrupted, it will surely cease to exist. In our body politic, each man is himself a constituent portion of the sovereign, and if the sovereign is to continue in power, he must continue to do right. When you here exercise your privileges at the ballot box, you are not only exercising a right, but you are also fulfilling a duty; and a heavy responsibility rests on you to fulfill your duty well. If you fail to work in public life, as well as in private, for honesty and uprightness and virtue, if you condone vice because the vicious man is smart, or if you in any other way cast your weight into the scales in favor of evil, you are just so far corrupting and making less valuable the birthright of your children. The duties of American citizenship are very solemn as well as very precious; and each one of us here today owes it to himself, to his children, and to all his fellow Americans, to show that he is capable of performing them in the right spirit. . . .

. . . All American citizens, whether born here or elsewhere, whether of one creed or another, stand on the same footing; we welcome every honest immigrant no matter from what country he comes, provided only that he leaves off his former nationality, and remains neither Celt nor Saxon, neither Frenchman nor German, but becomes an American, desirous of fulfilling in good faith the duties of American citizenship.

When we thus rule ourselves, we have the responsibilities of sovereigns, not of subjects. We must never exercise our rights either wickedly or thoughtlessly; we can continue to preserve them in but one possible way, by making the proper use of them.

THE DUTIES OF AMERICAN CITIZENSHIP

Of course, in one sense, the first essential for a man's being a good citizen is his possession of the home virtues of which we think when we call a man by the emphatic adjective of manly.[2] No man can be a good citizen who is not a good husband and a good father, who is not honest in his dealings with other men and women, faithful to his friends and fearless in the presence of his foes, who has not got a sound heart, a sound mind, and a sound body; exactly as no amount of attention to civic duties will save a nation if the domestic life is undermined, or there is lack of the rude military virtues which alone can assure a country's position in the world. In a free republic the ideal citizen must be one willing and able to take arms for the defense

[2] From an address to the Liberal Club, Buffalo, New York, January 26, 1893. In *The Liberal Club, Buffalo* [*Yearbook*], *1892–1893*, pp. 61–62, 64, 69–71.

of the flag, exactly as the ideal citizen must be the father of many healthy children. A race must be strong and vigorous; it must be a race of good fighters and good breeders, else its wisdom will come to naught and its virtue be ineffective; and no sweetness and delicacy, no love for and appreciation of beauty in art or literature, no capacity for building up material prosperity, can possibly atone for the lack of the great virile virtues.

. . . It ought to be axiomatic in this country that every man must devote a reasonable share of his time to doing his duty in the political life of the community. No man has a right to shirk his political duties under whatever plea of pleasure or business; and while such shirking may be pardoned in those of small means, it is entirely unpardonable in those among whom it is most common—in the people whose circumstances give them freedom in the struggle for life. . . .

The first duty of an American citizen, then, is that he shall work in politics; his second duty is that he shall do that work in a practical manner; and his third is that it shall be done in accord with the highest principles of honor and justice. . . .

I do wish that more of our good citizens would go into politics, and would do it in the same spirit with which their fathers went into the Federal armies. Begin with the little thing, and do not expect to accomplish anything without an effort. . . .

But in advising you to be practical and to work hard, I must not for one moment be understood as advising you to abandon one iota of your self-respect and devotion to principle. It is a bad sign for the country to see one class of our citizens sneer at practical politicians, and another at Sunday-school politics. No man can do both effective and decent work in public life unless he is a practical politician on the one hand, and a sturdy believer in Sunday-school politics on the other. He must always strive manfully for the best, and yet, like Abraham Lincoln, must often resign himself to accept the best possible.

GOOD VERSUS BAD CITIZENSHIP

The good citizen is the man who, whatever his wealth or his poverty, strives manfully to do his duty to himself, to his family, to his neighbor, to the State; who is incapable of the baseness which manifests itself either in arrogance or in envy, but who while demanding justice for himself is no less scrupulous to do justice to others.[3] It is

[3] From an address at the New York State Fair, Syracuse, September 7, 1903. In Willis Fletcher Johnson, ed., *Addresses and Papers of Theodore Roosevelt* (New York, 1909), pp. 163–64, 166–67.

because the average American citizen, rich or poor, is of just this type that we have cause for our profound faith in the future of the Republic.

Ours is a government of liberty, by, through, and under the law. Lawlessness and connivance at law-breaking—whether the law-breaking take the form of a crime of greed and cunning or of a crime of violence—are destructive not only of order, but of the true liberties which can only come through order. . . .

Let the watchwords of all our people be the old familiar watchwords of honesty, decency, fair-dealing and common sense. The qualities denoted by these words are essential to all of us as we deal with the complex industrial problems of to-day, the problems affecting not merely the accumulation but even more the wise distribution of wealth. . . .

Men sincerely interested in the due protection of property, and men sincerely interested in seeing that the just rights of labor are guaranteed, should alike remember not only that in the long run neither the capitalist nor the wage-worker can be helped in healthy fashion save by one helping the other; but also that to require either side to obey the law and do its full duty toward the community is emphatically to that side's real interest.

There is no worse enemy of the wage-worker than the man who condones mob violence in any shape or who preaches class hatred; and surely the slightest acquaintance with our industrial history should teach even the most shortsighted that the times of most suffering for our people as a whole, the times when business is stagnant, and capital suffers from shrinkage and gets no return from its investments, are exactly the times of hardship, and want, and grim disaster among the poor. . . .

In his turn the capitalist who is really a conservative, the man who has forethought as well as patriotism, should heartily welcome every effort, legislative or otherwise, which has for its object to secure fair dealing by capital, corporate or individual, toward the public and toward the employee. . . .

There is no room in our healthy American life for the mere idler, for the man or the woman whose object it is throughout life to shirk the duties which life ought to bring. Life can mean nothing worth meaning, unless its prime aim is the doing of duty, the achievement of results worth achieving. . . .

. . . To win success in the business world, to become a first-class mechanic, a successful farmer, an able lawyer or doctor, means that the man has devoted his best energy and power through long years to the achievement of his ends. So it is in the life of the family, upon which in the last analysis the whole welfare of the Nation rests. The

man or woman who as bread-winner and home-maker, or as wife and
mother, has done all that he or she can do, patiently and uncomplain-
ingly, is to be honored; and is to be envied by all those who have never
had the good fortune to feel the need and duty of doing such work.
The woman who has borne, and who has reared as they should be
reared, a family of children, has in the most emphatic manner deserved
well of the Republic.

CHARACTER

In a democracy like ours we cannot expect the stream to rise
higher than its source.[4] If the average man and the average woman are
not of the right type, your public men will not be of the right type.
The average man must be a decent man in his own home, he must pull
his own weight, he must be a decent neighbor, and a man with whom
you like to work and with whom you like to deal, or he cannot be a
good citizen. That is good as a beginning; but it is not enough. He
must show in his relations with his fellows and in his dealing with
the state the essentials of good citizenship. Genius is not necessary.
Genius is a fine thing; but fortunately character is not only more common, but better. What he needs to show is character, and there are
three essential qualities going to make up character.

In the first place, there is honesty. The bolder a man is the worse
he is, if he hasn't honesty. Don't be misled by that unfortunate trait
sometimes shown by our people—the trait of deifying mere smartness,
meaning thereby mental subtlety and ability unencumbered by any
sense of responsibility.

But honesty is not enough. I don't care how honest a man is, if he
is timid he is no good. I don't want to see a division of our citizenship
into good men who are afraid and bad men who are not at all afraid.
The honest man who is afraid is of just as little use in civic life as in
war.

You need honesty and then you need courage; but both of them
together are not enough. I don't care how honest a man is and how
brave he is; if he is a natural-born fool you can do nothing with him;
and perhaps this applies particularly to people in the profession of
politics. Of course, the bolder a politician is, if he is dishonest, the
worse he is, hunt him out of public life; and a feeble, well-meaning,
timid politician, like the other good, timid people, is of no use; but

[4] From a speech delivered in Milwaukee, September 7, 1910. Reprinted in
Theodore Roosevelt, *The New Nationalism*, with an Introduction and Notes by
William E. Leuchtenburg (Englewood Cliffs, N.J.: Prentice-Hall, Inc., 1961), pp.
141–42. Copyright 1961 by Prentice-Hall, Inc. Reprinted by permission of the
publisher.

the bold, incorruptible politician who stupidly goes wrong may be just as useless to a community in the long run as if he were hired by some dishonest man to do his work. So there is a third quality; that is, you must possess the saving grace of common sense.

5
The Martial Spirit

In the late 1890s Roosevelt found himself in a position to influence the formulation and execution of American foreign policy. He and a small group of expansionists in Washington had long chafed at what they regarded as a weak and insular national posture in foreign affairs. The mounting crisis over Cuba in 1897 and 1898 gave these advocates of a "larger" policy an opportunity to help set the nation on a new course. Assistant Secretary of the Navy Roosevelt worked assiduously to ready the fleet for war, and when war was finally declared, in April, 1898, nothing would do but for him to go to battle himself. To his immense satisfaction, he played the part gallantly and exhilarantly. The results of the Spanish-American War reinforced Roosevelt's conviction that the United States must expand, must assume new international duties, must play a larger role in the world. The documents that follow illustrate the Rough Rider's aggressive nationalism and jingoism in the 1890s, his "crowded hour" at San Juan Hill, and his ideas about peace, war, and overseas expansion around the turn of the century.

AN AGGRESSIVE FOREIGN POLICY

It is earnestly to be hoped that the Republican party will also make an aggressive fight on the question of America's foreign policy.[1] A policy of buncombe and spread-eagleism in foreign affairs would be sincerely to be deprecated; but a policy of tame submission to insult is even worse. . . .

We should build a first-class fighting navy—a navy, not of mere swift commerce-destroyers, but of powerful battleships. We should annex Hawaii immediately. It was a crime against the United States, it was a crime against white civilization, not to annex it two years and a half ago. The delay did damage that is perhaps irreparable; for it means that at the critical period of the island's growth the influx of population consisted, not of white Americans, but of low-caste laborers drawn from the yellow races. We should build the Isthmian Canal, and it should be built either by the United States Government or

[1] TR, "The Issues of 1896," *Century Magazine,* LI (November, 1895), 71–72.

under its protection. We should inform Great Britain, with equal firmness and courtesy, that the Monroe Doctrine is very much alive, and that the United States cannot tolerate the aggrandizement of a European power on American soil, especially when such aggrandizement takes the form of an attempt to seize the mouths of the Orinoco.

This does not mean a policy of bluster. No American President or secretary of state, no American legislative body, should ever make a threat which is not, if necessary, to be backed by force of arms. Honorable peace is always desirable, but under no circumstances should we permit ourselves to be defrauded of our just rights by any fear of war. No amount of material prosperity can atone for lack of national self-respect; and in no way can national self-respect be easier lost than through a peace obtained or preserved unworthily, whether through cowardice or through sluggish indifference.

"A GREAT CRISIS IS UPON US"

. . . Of course I cannot speak in public, but I have advised the President in the presence of his Cabinet, as well as Judge Day and Senator Hanna, as strongly as I knew how, to settle this matter instantly by armed intervention; and I told the President in the plainest language that no other course was compatible with our national honor, or with the claims of humanity on behalf of the wretched women and children of Cuba.[2] I am more grieved and indignant than I can say at there being any delay on our part in a matter like this. A great crisis is upon us, and if we do not rise level to it, we shall have spotted the pages of our history with a dark blot of shame.

*　　*　　*

. . . I do not want you to believe that if I go with the Army in the event of war I shall be acting in a mere spirit of levity or recklessness, or without having carefully thought out my duty according to my convictions.[3] . . .

In the first place my work here has been mainly one of preparation. In time of peace military men cannot speak to the civilian heads of the administration as I could, and did, speak, and I have been able to accomplish a good deal in getting the Navy ready. It is not of course in exactly the shape I should like to see it, but still it is in very good

[2] TR to William Sheffield Cowles, March 30, 1898. In Elting E. Morison and associates eds., *The Letters of Theodore Roosevelt*, 8 vols. (Cambridge: Harvard University Press, 1951–54), II, 804. Copyright 1951, 1952, 1954 by the President and Fellows of Harvard College. Reprinted by permission of the publisher.

[3] TR to Paul Dana, April 18, 1898. In Morison and associates, eds., *The Letters of Theodore Roosevelt*, II, 816–17. Reprinted by permission of the publisher.

shape indeed, and will respond nobly to any demand made upon it. Now, as I say, I have been useful in this work of preparation; but when the clash of arms comes the work of preparation will, for the most part, be done, and the task will be shifted to those whose duty it is to use aright the materials already prepared. . . . Very much of my usefulness during the past year has been due to the fact that I gave persistent expressions to the views of the best officers of the Department who could not otherwise have made themselves heard. In time of war these men will be heard without difficulty.

Secondly, I want to go because I wouldn't feel that I had been entirely true to my belief and convictions, and to the ideal I had set for myself if I didn't go. I don't want you to think that I am talking like a prig, for I know perfectly well that one never is able to analyze with entire accuracy all of one's motives. But I am entirely certain that I don't expect any military glory out of this Cuban war, more than what is implied in the honorable performance of duty. For two years I have consistently preached the doctrine of a resolute foreign policy, and of readiness to accept the arbitrament of the sword if necessary; and I have always intended to act up to my preaching if occasion arose. Now the occasion has arisen, and I ought to meet it. I have had, as you know, a perfect horror of the ideas which are perhaps most clearly crystalized in the editorials of papers like the *Evening Post*; that is, of the ideas of the peace-at-any-price theorists on the one side, the timid and scholarly men in whom refinement and culture have been developed at the expense of all the virile qualities; and a horror even greater of the big moneyed men in whose minds money and material prosperity have finally dwarfed everything else. . . . For two years I have been urging that we put Spain out of Cuba, and if there ever was a righteous war it will be this; and if, owing to the unfortunate delay in beginning it, we see our men dying of yellow fever in Cuba I should hate to be comfortably at home in Washington, although I have as much dislike of death as anyone could have, and take as keen enjoyment in life.

Moreover, an additional reason for my going is the fact that though I have a wife and six children, they are not dependent upon my exertions for support. I am not a rich man, and my children will have to work; but they will be well educated and comfortably brought up, and inasmuch as I have never been in a money-making pursuit my loss would not very materially affect their income.

THE ROUGH RIDER

I sent messenger after messenger to try to find General Sumner or General Wood and get permission to advance, and was just about making up my mind that in the absence of orders I had better "march toward the guns," when Lieutenant-Colonel Dorst came riding up through the storm of bullets with the welcome command "to move forward and support the regulars in the assault on the hills in front." [4] . . .

The instant I received the order I sprang on my horse and then my "crowded hour" began. . . . I formed my men in column of troops, each troop extended in open skirmishing order, the right resting on the wire fences which bordered the sunken lane. . . .

I soon found that I could get that line, behind which I personally was, faster forward than the one immediately in front of it, with the result that the two rearmost lines of the regiment began to crowd together; so I rode through them both, the better to move on the one in front. This happened with every line in succession, until I found myself at the head of the regiment. . . .

By the time I had come to the head of the regiment we ran into the left wing of the Ninth Regulars, and some of the First Regulars, who were lying down; that is, the troopers were lying down, while the officers were walking to and fro. . . .

I spoke to the captain in command of the rear platoons, saying that I had been ordered to support the regulars in the attack upon the hills, and that in my judgment we could not take these hills by firing at them, and that we must rush them. He answered that his orders were to keep his men lying where they were, and that he could not charge without orders. I asked where the colonel was, and as he was not in sight, said, "Then I am the ranking officer here and I give the order to charge"—for I did not want to keep the men longer in the open suffering under a fire which they could not effectively return. Naturally the captain hesitated to obey this order when no word had been received from his own colonel. So I said, "Then let my men through, sir," and rode on through the lines, followed by the grinning Rough Riders, whose attention had been completely taken off the Spanish bullets, partly by my dialogue with the regulars, and partly by the language I had been using to themselves as I got the lines forward, for I had been joking with some and swearing at others, as the exigencies of the case seemed to demand. When we started to go through, however, it proved too much for the regulars, and they jumped up and came along, their officers and troops mingling with mine, all being delighted at the chance. . . .

By this time we were all in the spirit of the thing and greatly excited by the charge, the men cheering and running forward between shots, while the delighted faces of the foremost officers . . . as they ran at

[4] Hermann Hagedorn, ed., *The Works of Theodore Roosevelt*, National Edition, 20 vols. (New York: Charles Scribner's Sons, 1926), XI, 80–89, 100. Copyright 1926 by Charles Scribner's Sons. Reprinted by permission of the publisher.

the head of their troops, will always stay in my mind. . . . Being on horseback I was, of course, able to get ahead of the men on foot, excepting my orderly, Henry Bardshar, who had run ahead very fast in order to get better shots at the Spaniards, who were now running out of the ranch buildings. . . . Some forty yards from the top I ran into a wire fence and jumped off little Texas, turning him loose. He had been scraped by a couple of bullets, one of which nicked my elbow, and I never expected to see him again. As I ran up to the hill, Bardshar stopped to shoot, and two Spaniards fell as he emptied his magazine. . . .

No sooner were we on the crest than the Spaniards from the line of hills in our front, where they were strongly intrenched, opened a very heavy fire upon us with their rifles. They also opened upon us with one or two pieces of artillery, using time fuses which burned very accurately, the shells exploding right over our heads. . . .

The infantry got nearer and nearer the crest of the hill. At last we could see the Spaniards running from the rifle-pits as the Americans came on in their final rush. Then I stopped my men for fear they should injure their comrades, and called to them to charge the next line of trenches, on the hills in our front, from which we had been undergoing a good deal of punishment. Thinking that the men would all come, I jumped over the wire fence in front of us and started at the double; but, as a matter of fact, the troopers were so excited, what with shooting and being shot, and shouting and cheering, that they did not hear, or did not heed me; and after running about a hundred yards I found I had only five men along with me. Bullets were ripping the grass all around us, and one of the men, Clay Green, was mortally wounded; another, Winslow Clark, a Harvard man, was shot first in the leg and then through the body. He made not the slightest murmur, only asking me to put his water canteen where he could get at it, which I did; he ultimately recovered. There was no use going on with the remaining three men, and I bade them stay where they were while I went back and brought up the rest of the brigade. This was a decidedly cool request, for there was really no possible point in letting them stay there while I went back; but at the moment it seemed perfectly natural to me, and apparently so to them, for they cheerfully nodded, and sat down in the grass, firing back at the line of trenches from which the Spaniards were shooting at them. Meanwhile, I ran back, jumped over the wire fence, and went over the crest of the hill, filled with anger against the troopers, and especially those of my own regiment, for not having accompanied me. They, of course, were quite innocent of wrong-doing; and even while I taunted them bitterly for not having followed me, it was all I could do not to smile at the look of injury and surprise that came over their faces, while they cried out: "We didn't hear you, we didn't see you go, Colonel; lead on now, we'll sure follow you." I wanted the other regiments to come too, so I ran down to where General Sumner was and asked him if I might make the charge; and he told me to go and that he would see that the men followed. By this time everybody had his attention attracted, and when I leaped over the fence again, with Major Jenkins beside me, the men of the various regiments which were already on the hill came with a rush, and we started across the wide valley which lay between us and the Spanish intrenchments. . . . The long-legged men like Greenway, Goodrich, Sharp-shooter Proffit, and others, outstripped the rest of us, as we had a considerable distance to go. Long before we got near them the Spaniards ran, save a few here and there, who either surrendered or were shot down. When we reached the trenches we found them filled with dead bodies in the light blue and white uniform of the Spanish regular army. There were very few wounded. Most of the fallen had little holes in their heads from which their brains were oozing; for they were covered from the neck down by the trenches. . . .

In this fight our regiment had numbered four hundred and ninety men, as, in addition to the killed and wounded of the first fight, some had had to go to the hospital for sickness and some had been left behind with the baggage, or were detailed on other duty. Eighty-nine were killed and wounded: the heaviest loss suffered by any regiment in the cavalry division. The Spaniards made a stiff fight, standing firm until we charged home. They fought much more stubbornly than at Las Guasimas. We ought to have expected this, for they have always done well in holding intrenchments. On this day they showed themselves to be brave foes, worthy of honor for their gallantry.

EXPANSION AND PEACE

. . . Peace is a great good; and doubly harmful, therefore, is the attitude of those who advocate it in terms that would make it synonymous with selfish and cowardly shrinking from warring against the existence of evil.[5] The wisest and most far-seeing champions of peace will ever remember that, in the first place, to be good it must be righteous—for unrighteous and cowardly peace may be worse than any war—and, in the second place, that it can often be obtained only at the cost of war. . . .

Again, peace may only come through war. There are men in our country who seemingly forget that at the outbreak of the Civil War the great cry raised by the opponents of the war was the cry for peace. . . .

Wars between civilized communities are very dreadful, and as na-

[5] TR, "Expansion and Peace," *The Independent*, LI (December 21, 1899), 3401–4.

tions grow more and more civilized, we have every reason, not merely to hope, but to believe that they will grow rarer and rarer. Even with civilized peoples, as was shown by our own experience in 1861, it may be necessary at last to draw the sword rather than to submit to wrongdoing. But a very marked feature in the world history of the present century has been the growing infrequency of wars between great civilized nations. The Peace Conference at The Hague is but one of the signs of this growth. . . .

The growth of peacefulness between nations, however, has been confined strictly to those that are civilized. It can only come when both parties to a possible quarrel feel the same spirit. With a barbarous nation peace is the exceptional condition. On the border between civilization and barbarism war is generally normal because it must be under the conditions of barbarism. . . .

. . . This has been the case in every instance of expansion during the present century, whether the expanding power were France or England, Russia or America. In every instance the expansion has been of benefit, not so much to the Power nominally benefited, as to the whole world. In every instance the result proved that the expanding Power was doing a duty to civilization far greater and more important than could have been done by any stationary Power. Take the case of France and Algiers. During the early decades of the present century piracy of the most dreadful description was rife in the Mediterranean, and thousands of civilized men were yearly dragged into slavery by the Moorish pirates. A degrading peace was purchased by the civilized Powers by the payment of tribute. Our own country was one among the tributary nations which thus paid blood money to the Moslem bandits of the sea. We fought occasional battles with them; and so on a larger scale did the English. But peace did not follow, because the country was not occupied. Our last payment was made in 1830, and the reason it was the last was because in that year the French conquest of Algiers began. Foolish sentimentalists, like those who wrote little poems in favor of the Mahdists against the English, and who now write little essays in favor of Aguinaldo against the Americans, celebrated the Algerian freebooters as heroes who were striving for liberty against the invading French. But the French continued to do their work; France expanded over Algiers, and the result was that piracy in the Mediterranean came to an end, and Algiers has thriven as never before in its history. On an even larger scale the same thing is true of England and the Sudan. . . . Above all, there has been the greatest possible gain in peace. The rule of law and of order has succeeded to the rule of barbarous and bloody violence. Until the great civilized nations stepped in there was no chance for anything but such bloody violence.

So it has been in the history of our own country. Of course our whole national history has been one of expansion. . . . In North America, as elsewhere throughout the entire world, the expansion of a civilized nation has invariably meant the growth of the area in which peace is normal throughout the world.

The same will be true of the Philippines. If the men who have counseled national degradation, national dishonor, by urging us to leave the Philippines and put the Aguinaldan oligarchy in control of those islands could have their way, we should merely turn them over to rapine and bloodshed until some stronger, manlier power stepped in to do the task we had shown ourselves fearful of performing. But as it is this country will keep the islands and will establish therein a stable and orderly government, so that one more fair spot of the world's surface shall have been snatched from the forces of darkness. Fundamentally the cause of expansion is the cause of peace. . . .

It is only the warlike power of a civilized people that can give peace to the world.

6

The Presidency
and Domestic Issues

As our first modern chief executive, TR contributed substantially to the revitalization of the presidency. He early perceived the potential role of the strong executive in responding to the needs of a society undergoing rapid change. While lacking an elaborate theory to direct and justify positive government and a powerful presidency, he moved intuitively and skillfully to strengthen the policies emanating from Washington and to expand the influence of his office. He made himself master of his party, involved himself fully in the difficult task of achieving efficient administration, demonstrated how public opinion could be mobilized in support of presidential policies, and suggested ways in which the president could succeed as a legislative leader. The selections reprinted here deal with Roosevelt's major policies in the domestic sphere and throw light on his view of the presidency as well as on the means by which he sought to achieve his goals.

THE REGULATION OF BUSINESS

In my Message to the present Congress at its first session I discussed at length the question of the regulation of those big corporations commonly doing an interstate business, often with some tendency to monopoly, which are popularly known as trusts.[1] The experience of the past year has emphasized, in my opinion, the desirability of the steps I then proposed. A fundamental requisite of social efficiency is a high standard of individual energy and excellence; but this is in no wise inconsistent with power to act in combination for aims which can not so well be achieved by the individual acting alone. A fundamental base of civilization is the inviolability of property; but this is in no wise inconsistent with the right of society to regulate the exercise of the artificial powers which it confers upon the owners of prop-

[1] From the annual message to Congress, December 2, 1902. In James D. Richardson, ed., *A Compilation of the Messages and Papers of the Presidents, 1789–1904,* 10 vols. (New York: Bureau of National Literature and Art, 1904), X, 512–14. Later selections from Volume X of this work are taken from the edition of 1904.

erty, under the name of corporate franchises, in such a way as to prevent the misuse of these powers. Corporations, and especially combinations of corporations, should be managed under public regulation. Experience has shown that under our system of government the necessary supervision can not be obtained by State action. It must therefore be achieved by national action. Our aim is not to do away with corporations; on the contrary, these big aggregations are an inevitable development of modern industrialism, and the effort to destroy them would be futile unless accomplished in ways that would work the utmost mischief to the entire body politic. We can do nothing of good in the way of regulating and supervising these corporations until we fix clearly in our minds that we are not attacking the corporations, but endeavoring to do away with any evil in them. We are not hostile to them; we are merely determined that they shall be so handled as to subserve the public good. We draw the line against misconduct, not against wealth. The capitalist who, alone or in conjunction with his fellows, performs some great industrial feat by which he wins money is a welldoer, not a wrongdoer, provided only he works in proper and legitimate lines. We wish to favor such a man when he does well. We wish to supervise and control his actions only to prevent him from doing ill. Publicity can do no harm to the honest corporation; and we need not be overtender about sparing the dishonest corporation. . . .

No more important subject can come before the Congress than this of the regulation of interstate business. This country can not afford to sit supine on the plea that under our peculiar system of government we are helpless in the presence of the new conditions, and unable to grapple with them or to cut out whatever of evil has arisen in connection with them. The power of the Congress to regulate interstate commerce is an absolute and unqualified grant, and without limitations other than those prescribed by the Constitution. The Congress has constitutional authority to make all laws necessary and proper for executing this power, and I am satisfied that this power has not been exhausted by any legislation now on the statute books. It is evident, therefore, that evils restrictive of commercial freedom and entailing restraint upon national commerce fall within the regulative power of the Congress, and that a wise and reasonable law would be a necessary and proper exercise of Congressional authority to the end that such evils should be eradicated.

*　　*　　*

The present Congress has taken long strides in the direction of securing proper supervision and control by the National Government over corporations engaged in interstate business—and the enormous majority of corporations of any size are engaged in interstate business.[2] The passage of the railway-rate bill, and only to a less degree the passage of the pure-food bill, and the provision for increasing and rendering more effective national control over the beef-packing industry, mark an important advance in the proper direction. . . .

It must not be supposed, however, that with the passage of these laws it will be possible to stop progress along the line of increasing the power of the National Government over the use of capital in interstate commerce. For example, there will ultimately be need of enlarging the powers of the Interstate Commerce Commission along several different lines, so as to give it a larger and more efficient control over the railroads.

It cannot too often be repeated that experience has conclusively shown the impossibility of securing by the actions of nearly half a hundred different State legislatures anything but ineffective chaos in the way of dealing with the great corporations which do not operate exclusively within the limits of any one State. . . . The best way to avert the very undesirable move for the government ownership of railways is to secure by the government on behalf of the people as a whole such adequate control and regulation of the great interstate common carriers as will do away with the evils which give rise to the agitation against them. So the proper antidote to the dangerous and wicked agitation against the men of wealth as such is to secure by proper legislation and executive action the abolition of the grave abuses which actually do obtain in connection with the business use of wealth under our present system—or rather no system—of failure to exercise any adequate control at all. Some persons speak as if the exercise of such governmental control would do away with the freedom of individual initiative and dwarf individual effort. This is not a fact. It would be a veritable calamity to fail to put a premium upon individual initiative, individual capacity and effort; upon the energy, character, and foresight which it is so important to encourage in the individual. But as a matter of fact the deadening and degrading effect of pure socialism, and especially of its extreme form, communism, and the destruction of individual character which they would bring about, are in part achieved by the wholly unregulated competition which results in a single individual or corporation rising at the expense of all others until his or its rise effectually checks all competition and reduces former competitors to a position of utter inferiority and subordination.

* * *

. . . The amount of money the representatives of certain great

[2] From the annual message to Congress, December 4, 1906. In James D. Richardson, ed., *A Compilation of the Messages and Papers of the Presidents* . . . , rev. ed., 11 vol. (New York: Bureau of National Literature and Art, 1911), X, 7418–20.

moneyed interests are willing to spend can be gauged by their recent publication broadcast throughout the papers of this country, from the Atlantic to the Pacific, of huge advertisements attacking with envenomed bitterness the administration's policy of warning against successful dishonesty, and by their circulation of pamphlets and books prepared with the same object; while they likewise push the circulation of the writings and speeches of men, who, whether because they are misled, or because, seeing the light, they yet are willing to sin against the light, serve these their masters of great wealth to the cost of the plain people.[3] . . . From the railroad rate law to the pure food law, every measure for honesty in business that has been passed during the last six years has been opposed by these men on its passage and in its administration with every resource that bitter and unscrupulous craft could suggest and the command of almost unlimited money secure. But for the last year the attack has been made with most bitterness upon the actual administration of the law, especially through the Department of Justice, but also through the Interstate Commerce Commission and the Bureau of Corporations. The extraordinary violence of the assaults upon our policy contained in these speeches, editorials, articles, advertisements and pamphlets, and the enormous sums of money spent in these various ways, give a fairly accurate measure of the anger and terror which our public actions have caused the corrupt men of vast wealth to feel in the very marrow of their being. . . .

Much is said in these attacks upon the policy of the present administration, about the rights of "innocent stockholders." That stockholder is not innocent who voluntarily purchases stock in a corporation whose methods and management he knows to be corrupt, and stockholders are bound to try to secure honest management, or else are estopped from complaining about the proceedings the government finds necessary in order to compel the corporation to obey the law. There has been in the past grave wrong done innocent stockholders by overcapitalization, stock watering, stock jobbing, stock manipulation. This we have sought to prevent—first, by exposing the thing done and punishing the offender when any existing law had been violated; second, by recommending the passage of laws which would make unlawful similar practices for the future. . . .

The "business" which is hurt by the movement for honesty is the kind of business which, in the long run it pays the country to have hurt. It is the kind of business which has tended to make the very name "high finance" a term of scandal, to which all honest American men of business should join in putting an end. . . .

[3] From a special message to Congress, January 31, 1908. In Willis Fletcher Johnson, ed., *Addresses and Papers of Theodore Roosevelt* (New York, 1909), pp. 415–16, 418, 420, 424–25.

I do not for a moment believe that the actions of this administration have brought on business distress; so far as this is due to local and not world-wide causes, and to the actions of any particular individuals, it is due to the speculative folly and flagrant dishonesty of a few men of great wealth, who seek to shield themselves from the effects of their own wrongdoing by ascribing its results to the actions of those who have sought to put a stop to the wrongdoing. But if it were true that to cut out rottenness from the body politic meant a momentary check to an unhealthy seeming prosperity, I should not for one moment hesitate to put the knife to the corruption. On behalf of all our people, on behalf no less of the honest man of means than of the honest man who earns each day's livelihood by that day's sweat of his brow, it is necessary to insist upon honesty in business and politics alike, in all walks of life, in big things and in little things; upon just and fair dealings as between man and man.

LABOR AND THE SQUARE DEAL

How to secure fair treatment alike for labor and for capital, how to hold in check the unscrupulous man, whether employer or employee, without weakening individual initiative, without hampering and cramping the industrial development of the country, is a problem fraught with great difficulties and one which it is of the highest importance to solve on lines of sanity and far-sighted common sense as well as of devotion to the right.[4] This is an era of federation and combination. Exactly as business men find they must often work through corporations, and as it is a constant tendency of these corporations to grow larger, so it is often necessary for laboring men to work in federations, and these have become important factors of modern industrial life. Both kinds of federation, capitalistic and labor, can do much good, and as a necessary corollary they can both do evil. . . . Each must refrain from arbitrary or tyrannous interference with the rights of others. Organized capital and organized labor alike should remember that in the long run the interest of each must be brought into harmony with the interest of the general public; and the conduct of each must conform to the fundamental rules of obedience to the law, of individual freedom, and of justice and fair dealing toward all. Each should remember that in addition to power it must strive after the realization of healthy, lofty, and generous ideals. Every employer, every wage-worker, must be guaranteed his liberty and his right to do as he likes with his property or his labor so long as he does not infringe upon the rights of others. . . . Above

[4] From the annual message to Congress, December 2, 1902. In Richardson, ed., *Messages and Papers of the Presidents*, X, 517–18.

all, we need to remember that any kind of class animosity in the political world is, if possible, even more wicked, even more destructive to national welfare, than sectional, race, or religious animosity. We can get good government only upon condition that we keep true to the principles upon which this Nation was founded, and judge each man not as a part of a class, but upon his individual merits.

* * *

Many of these strikes and lockouts would not have occurred had the parties to the dispute been required to appear before an unprejudiced body representing the nation and, face to face, state the reasons for their contention.[5] In most instances the dispute would doubtless be found to be due to a misunderstanding by each of the other's rights, aggravated by an unwillingness of either party to accept as true the statements of the other as to the justice or injustice of the matters in dispute. The exercise of a judicial spirit by a disinterested body representing the Federal Government, such as would be provided by a commission on conciliation and arbitration, would tend to create an atmosphere of friendliness and conciliation between contending parties; and the giving each side an equal opportunity to present fully its case in the presence of the other would prevent many disputes from developing into serious strikes or lockouts, and, in other cases, would enable the commission to persuade the opposing parties to come to terms.

In this age of great corporate and labor combinations, neither employers nor employees should be left completely at the mercy of the stronger party to a dispute, regardless of the righteousness of their respective claims. The proposed measure would be in the line of securing recognition of the fact that in many strikes the public has itself an interest which cannot wisely be disregarded; an interest not merely of general convenience, for the question of a just and proper public policy must also be considered. In all legislation of this kind it is well to advance cautiously, testing each step by the actual results; the step proposed can surely be safely taken, for the decisions of the commission would not bind the parties in legal fashion, and yet would give a chance for public opinion to crystallize and thus to exert its full force for the right.

* * *

The National Government should be a model employer.[6] It should demand the highest quality of service from each of its employees and

[5] From the annual message to Congress, December 4, 1906. In Richardson, ed., *Messages and Papers of the Presidents*, rev. ed., X, 7417. Roosevelt was here recommending the establishment of a federal arbitration commission.

[6] From the annual message to Congress, December 4, 1907. In Richardson, ed., *Messages and Papers of the Presidents*, rev. ed., X, 7467–68.

it should care for all of them properly in return. Congress should adopt legislation providing limited but definite compensation for accidents to all workmen within the scope of the Federal power, including employees of navy-yards and arsenals. In other words, a model employers' liability act, far-reaching and thoroughgoing, should be enacted which should apply to all positions, public and private, over which the National Government has jurisdiction. . . .

. . . The number of accidents to wage-workers, including those that are preventable and those that are not, has become appalling in the mechanical, manufacturing, and transportation operations of the day. It works grim hardship to the ordinary wage-worker and his family to have the effect of such an accident fall solely upon him; and, on the other hand, there are whole classes of attorneys who exist only by inciting men who may or may not have been wronged to undertake suits for negligence. As a matter of fact a suit for negligence is generally an inadequate remedy for the person injured, while it often causes altogether disproportionate annoyance to the employer. The law should be made such that the payment for accidents by the employer would be automatic instead of being a matter for lawsuits. Workmen should receive certain and definite compensation for all accidents in industry irrespective of negligence. The employer is the agent of the public and on his own responsibility and for his own profit he serves the public. When he starts in motion agencies which create risks for others, he should take all the ordinary and extraordinary risks involved; and the risk he thus at the moment assumes will ultimately be assumed, as it ought to be, by the general public. Only in this way can the shock of the accident be diffused, instead of falling upon the man or woman least able to bear it, as is now the case. The community at large should share the burdens as well as the benefits of industry. . . .

. . . The practice of putting the entire burden of loss of life or limb upon the victim or the victim's family is a form of social injustice in which the United States stands in unenviable prominence. In both our Federal and State legislation we have, with few exceptions, scarcely gone farther than the repeal of the fellow-servant principle of the old law of liability, and in some of our States even this slight modification of a completely outgrown principle has not yet been secured. The legislation of the rest of the industrial world stands out in striking contrast to our backwardness in this respect.

THE DANGERS OF MUCKRAKING

. . . In "Pilgrim's Progress" the Man with the Muck-Rake is set forth as the example of him whose vision is fixed on carnal instead of on spiritual things.[7] Yet he also typifies the man who in this life consistently refuses to see aught that is lofty, and fixes his eyes with solemn intentness only on that which is vile and debasing. Now, it is very necessary that we should not flinch from seeing what is vile and debasing. There is filth on the floor, and it must be scraped up with the muck-rake; and there are times and places where this service is the most needed of all the services that can be performed. But the man who never does anything else, who never thinks or speaks or writes save of his feats with the muck-rake, speedily becomes, not a help to society, not an incitement to good, but one of the most potent forces for evil.

There are in the body politic, economic and social, many and grave evils, and there is urgent necessity for the sternest war upon them. There should be relentless exposure of and attack upon every evil man, whether politician or business man, every evil practice, whether in politics, in business or in social life. . . .

Any excess is almost sure to invite a reaction, and, unfortunately, the reaction, instead of taking the form of punishment of those guilty of the excess, is very apt to take the form either of punishment of the unoffending or of giving immunity, and even strength, to offenders. The effort to make financial or political profit out of the destruction of character can only result in public calamity. Gross and reckless assaults on character—whether on the stump or in newspaper, magazine or book—create a morbid and vicious public sentiment, and at the same time act as a profound deterrent to able men of normal sensitiveness and tend to prevent them from entering the public service at any price. . . .

. . . Expose the crime and hunt down the criminal; but remember that even in the case of crime, if it is attacked in sensational, lurid and untruthful fashion, the attack may do more damage to the public mind than the crime itself. It is because I feel that there should be no rest in the endless war against the forces of evil that I ask that the war be conducted with sanity as well as with resolution. The men with the muck-rakes are often indispensable to the well-being of society, but only if they know when to stop raking the muck, and to look upward to the celestial crown above them, to the crown of worthy endeavor. . . .

To assail the great and admitted evils of our political and industrial life with such crude and sweeping generalizations as to include decent men in the general condemnation means the searing of the public conscience. There results a general attitude either of cynical belief in and indifference to public corruption or else of a distrustful

[7] From an address at Washington, D.C., April 14, 1906. In Johnson, ed., *Addresses and Papers of Theodore Roosevelt*, pp. 311–16.

inability to discriminate between the good and the bad. Either attitude is fraught with untold damage to the country as a whole. . . .

. . . At this moment we are passing through a period of great unrest—social, political and industrial unrest. It is of the utmost importance for our future that this should prove to be not the unrest of mere rebelliousness against life, of mere dissatisfaction with the inevitable inequality of conditions, but the unrest of a resolute and eager ambition to secure the betterment of the individual and the nation. So far as this movement of agitation throughout the country takes the form of a fierce discontent with evil, of a determination to punish the authors of evil, whether in industry or politics, the feeling is to be heartily welcomed as a sign of healthy life.

If, on the other hand, it turns into a mere crusade of appetite against appetite, of a contest between the brutal greed of the "have-nots" and the brutal greed of the "haves," then it has no significance for good, but only for evil. If it seeks to establish a line of cleavage, not along the line which divides good men from bad, but along that other line, running at right angles thereto, which divides those who are well off from those who are less well off, then it will be fraught with immeasurable harm to the body politic.

CONSERVATION

Public opinion throughout the United States has moved steadily toward a just appreciation of the value of forests, whether planted or of natural growth.[8] The great part played by them in the creation and maintenance of the national wealth is now more fully realized than ever before.

Wise forest protection does not mean the withdrawal of forest resources, whether of wood, water, or grass, from contributing their full share to the welfare of the people, but, on the contrary, gives the assurance of larger and more certain supplies. The fundamental idea of forestry is the perpetuation of forests by use. Forest protection is not an end of itself; it is a means to increase and sustain the resources of our country and the industries which depend upon them. The preservation of our forests is an imperative business necessity. We have come to see clearly that whatever destroys the forest, except to make way for agriculture, threatens our well-being. . . .

The wise administration of the forest reserves will be not less helpful to the interests which depend on water than to those which depend on wood and grass. The water supply itself depends upon the

---

[8] From the annual message to Congress, December 3, 1901. In Richardson, ed., *Messages and Papers of the Presidents*, X, 431–35.

forest. In the arid region it is water, not land, which measures production. The western half of the United States would sustain a population greater than that of our whole country to-day if the waters that now run to waste were saved and used for irrigation. The forest and water problems are perhaps the most vital internal questions of the United States.

Certain of the forest reserves should also be made preserves for the wild forest creatures. All of the reserves should be better protected from fires. . . .

. . . The forest reserves should be set apart forever for the use and benefit of our people as a whole and not sacrificed to the short-sighted greed of a few.

The forests are natural reservoirs. By restraining the streams in flood and replenishing them in drought they make possible the use of waters otherwise wasted. They prevent the soil from washing, and so protect the storage reservoirs from filling up with silt. Forest conservation is therefore an essential condition of water conservation.

The forests alone cannot, however, fully regulate and conserve the waters of the arid region. Great storage works are necessary to equalize the flow of streams and to save the flood waters. Their construction has been conclusively shown to be an undertaking too vast for private effort. Nor can it be best accomplished by the individual States acting alone. Far-reaching interstate problems are involved; and the resources of single States would often be inadequate. It is properly a national function, at least in some of its features. It is as right for the National Government to make the streams and rivers of the arid region useful by engineering works for water storage as to make useful the rivers and harbors of the humid region by engineering works of another kind. . . .

The Government should construct and maintain these reservoirs as it does other public works. Where their purpose is to regulate the flow of streams, the water should be turned freely into the channels in the dry season to take the same course under the same laws as the natural flow.

The reclamation of the unsettled arid public lands presents a different problem. Here it is not enough to regulate the flow of streams. The object of the Government is to dispose of the land to settlers who will build homes upon it. To accomplish this object water must be brought within their reach.

The pioneer settlers on the arid public domain chose their homes along streams from which they could themselves divert the water to reclaim their holdings. Such opportunities are practically gone. There remain, however, vast areas of public land which can be made available for homestead settlement, but only by reservoirs and main-line canals impracticable for private enterprise. These irrigation works should be built by the National Government. . . .

. . . No reservoir or canal should ever be built to satisfy selfish personal or local interests; but only in accordance with the advice of trained experts, after long investigation has shown the locality where all the conditions combine to make the work most needed and fraught with the greatest usefulness to the community as a whole. There should be no extravagance, and the believers in the need of irrigation will most benefit their cause by seeing to it that it is free from the least taint of excessive or reckless expenditure of the public moneys.

* * *

. . . Planned and orderly development is essential to the best use of every natural resource, and to none more than to the best use of our inland waterways.[9] In the case of the waterways it has been conspicuously absent. Because such foresight was lacking, the interests of our rivers have been in fact overlooked, in spite of the immense sums spent upon them. It is evident that their most urgent need is a far-sighted and comprehensive plan, dealing not with navigation alone, nor with irrigation alone, but considering our inland waterways as a whole, and with reference to every use to which they can be put. The central motive of such a plan should be to get from the streams of the United States not only the fullest but also the most permanent service they are capable of rendering to the Nation as a whole. . . .

Citizens of all portions of the country are coming to realize that, however important the improvement of navigation may be, it is only one of many ends to be kept in view. The demand for navigation is hardly more pressing than the demands for reclaiming lands by irrigation in the arid regions and by drainage in the humid lowlands, or for utilizing the water-power now running to waste, or for purifying the waters so as to reduce or remove the tax of soil waste to promote manufactures and safeguard life. It is the part of wisdom to adopt not a jumble of unrelated plans, but a single comprehensive scheme for meeting all the demands so far as possible at the same time and by the same means. This is the reason why the Inland Waterways Commission was created in March last, largely in response to petitions from citizens of the interior, including many of the members of this Congress. Broad instructions were given to the Com-

[9] From an address delivered in Memphis, Tennessee, before the Deep Waterway Convention, October 4, 1907. In *The Roosevelt Policy: Speeches, Letters and State Papers, relating to Corporate Wealth and Closely Allied Topics, of Theodore Roosevelt, President of the United States,* 2 vols. (New York, 1908), II, 621, 625–26.

mission in accordance with this general policy that no plan should be prepared for the use of any stream for a single purpose without carefully considering, and so far as practicable actually providing for, the use of that stream for every other purpose. Plans for navigation and power should provide with special care for sites and terminals not only for the immediate present but also for the future. It is because of my conviction in these matters that I am here. The Inland Waterways Commission has a task broader than the consideration of waterways alone. There is an intimate relation between our streams and the development and conservation of all the other great permanent sources of wealth. It is not possible rightly to consider the one without the other. No study of the problem of the waterways could hope to be successful which failed to consider also the remaining factors in the great problem of conserving all our resources. Accordingly, I have asked the Waterways Commission to take account of the orderly development and conservation, not alone of the waters, but also of the soil, the forests, the mines, and all the other natural resources of our country.

THE SOUTH AND THE NEGRO

. . . I have always felt that the passage of the Fifteenth Amendment at the time it was passed was a mistake; but to admit this is very different from admitting that it is wise, even if it were practicable, now to repeal that amendment. . . . [10] I again agree with you that, as conditions are now, at this time, it is unwise and would do damage rather than good to press for its active enforcement by any means that Congress has at its command. But it is out of the question that there can be permanent acquiescence on the part of the North in an arrangement under which Mr. John Sharp Williams, the leader of the minority in the House, as compared with Mr. Cannon, the Speaker, elected by the majority, has just four times the political weight to which he is entitled. Mr. Williams represents a district in which there are three blacks to one white. It is an outrage that this one white man should first be allowed to suppress the votes of the three black men, and then to cast them himself in order to make his own vote equal to that of four men in Mr. Cannon's district. If this result came about as a natural effect of a genuine and honest effort to enforce an illiteracy test, or something of the sort, I believe there would be little or no objection to it in the North, in spite of the damage done the

[10] TR to Henry Smith Pritchett, December 14, 1904. In Elting E. Morison and associates, eds., *The Letters of Theodore Roosevelt*, 8 vols. (Cambridge: Harvard University Press, 1951–54), IV, 1066–71. Copyright 1951, 1952, 1954 by the President and Fellows of Harvard College. Reprinted by permission of the publisher.

North thereby; for I believe that the North has hearty sympathy with the trials of the South and is generously glad to assist the South whenever the South does not render it impossible by "superfluity of naughtiness." The trouble is that there is no such genuine law, and that there is no white man from a southern district in which blacks are numerous who does not tell you, either defiantly or as a joke, that any white man is allowed to vote, no matter how ignorant and degraded, and that the negro vote is practically suppressed because it *is* the negro vote. . . .

Now, about your proposition "to throw upon the states themselves the responsibility for dealing with the negro, subject only to the criticism of the other states, of England, and of the civilized world." Here I am able to speak of my positive knowledge. If I had adopted such a policy in its entirety during the last two years, slavery would be at this moment re-established in the guise of peonage in portions of Mississippi, Alabama and Georgia. The State courts and State officials positively refused to touch the question, and it grew up under State laws and the administration of State laws. I have partially broken it up by the action of the United States district attorneys and the United States courts. In each case I took a southerner, and usually a Democrat, as the agent through whom to work; and it is to these men—notably Judge Jones, whom I appointed in Alabama as a district judge—that the credit for the work is mainly due. But it would not have been done if I had thrown upon the States themselves the responsibility for dealing with the negro, subject only to outside criticism. The Federal Government must continue to exercise its functions in the South, just as it does in any other community.

. . . As a whole the southerners do demand, in effect, just precisely this: that is, the entire exclusion of negroes from office. Of course their best men do not demand it; but taken as a whole this is the demand they make; and their cry against me, aside from their hysterics over the Booker Washington incident, has been due to my acting just exactly as in this sentence you say they would not object to my acting. In almost every case I have had the approval and endorsement of the best whites; the better sentiment of the South has been with me, but it has been cowed and overborne by the violence of the men who seem to furnish almost all their leadership, alike in politics and in the press. You cannot find an intelligent and honest southerner who will not tell you that my appointees in the Southern States, taken as a whole, are better on the average even than Mr. Cleveland's; and a smaller percentage of them are negroes than was the case under Mr. McKinley; while these negroes are without an exception reputable and decent citizens and efficient officers. . . . But their knowledge and private acceptance of the truth of this fact has not prevented the southern leaders as a whole from inflaming their people well-nigh to madness by the coarsest form of personal vituperation of me, and by the most brazen mendacity as to what had been done.

The trouble is, my dear Mr. Pritchett, that in the last three years I really have tried exactly the course that you recommend, and the entire blame rests with the South for failure to meet my effort half way, or even one quarter, or one-tenth, or one-hundredth way. The North has not been to blame in the least. The northern newspapers and northern politicians have shown an extraordinary generosity in refusing to attack the South. The attack has come purely from the Vardamans, the Tillmans, the Senator Morgans, the John Sharp Williamses, and the like.

Let me illustrate what I mean by the concrete instance of the State of Mississippi. Mississippi is a Gulf State, and my foreign policy has been especially advantageous to the Gulf States, by the action taken as regards the Panama Canal, the Venezuela business, etc., etc. She is prosperous under our internal administration. So that the policies of the Government on general matters had been to Mississippi's great advantage. As regards the negro, Congress has done literally nothing during these three years, and has threatened literally nothing—for the present agitation about the enforcement of the Fourteenth Amendment was caused by, and did not in the least cause, the violent southern outburst of the last three years. In Mississippi I found the Republican organization such a worthless body that I absolutely threw it aside. I made almost all my appointments from among Democrats. . . . This fact is invariably admitted by the best Mississippi papers, and not a Senator or Congressman from Mississippi has complained to me of the character of a single officeholder, although I have invited them to do so if there were any complaints to make. Of the very few negro appointments, most were to small post offices in the black belt in villages where there were only negroes, and where therefore a negro had to be appointed. Lastly, I somewhat diminished the number of officeholders who were negroes; so that the proportion, which was insignificant even under McKinley, has been still further reduced. Not a colored man was appointed save after securing his endorsement by all the best white people of the vicinity.

Yet this is the State which elected Vardaman, partly because of his foul-mouthed abuse of me, and which has gone into hysterics against me absolutely without one little particle of excuse. This is the state in which the respectable people of Indianola permitted the mob to run out the colored postmistress who had been originally appointed by President McKinley, and then reappointed by President McKinley at the end of her first term, with the approval of the two Democratic United States Senators. She was recommended by all the best white people of the town, and her bondsmen included the two bankers of the town, the then Democratic State Senator and the ex-Democratic State Senator. She and her husband were cultivated, intelligent people, very modest and unassuming, and were taxpayers, being well up among the better-off people of the town. From motives which I have never been able to fathom the hoodlum element decided to run her out. They did so, and the best people of the town first, and then the whole State, instead of acting as you have said you believe the southerners under such conditions would act, turned in at once to support the infamous scoundrels who had been guilty of the offense. There were of course a few good men who protested, but they counted for nothing in the general torrent. It was Vardaman who gave utterance to the real feeling of the State on the subject.

Mind you, this is what happened exactly under the conditions that you suppose would bring about good results. I had abandoned all effort to do anything through the Republican party in Mississippi. I was acting through Democrats, southerners, ex-Confederates, who were men of high character and proved governmental ability, and of good repute in the community. Congress was proceeding upon the plan of entire noninterference with the South, and of leaving them to do as they wished save as they might be influenced by outside criticism. The result shows that the chief, and in fact the all-important, element of trouble was the folly and wickedness of the mass of the present leaders of the southern whites. . . .

. . . It may be that it would have been better for me not to have had Booker Washington at dinner. It may be that it would have been better not to have originally nominated Crum for the Charleston collectorship. Personally I think I was right in both instances. But even if I was wrong, to say that the South's attitude is explained by these two acts is to say that the South is in a condition of violent chronic hysteria.

7
International Policies

Roosevelt's leadership in foreign affairs was perhaps even more significant than his performance in the arena of domestic politics. He relished the powerful role he played in the conduct of American foreign policy, and his administration was easily the most active in world affairs of any president since the Civil War. Roosevelt's views on international questions reflected a blend of idealism, romanticism, and realism. His basic convictions, as William H. Harbaugh has pointed out, were these: (1) self-defense was the first imperative of organized society; (2) the interests of highly civilized peoples took precedence over those of backward peoples; and (3) advanced peoples were morally obligated to support the onward march of civilization.[1] As a diplomatist TR exemplified Machiavelli's belief that the successful prince must be capable of acting both like a lion and a fox. The twenty-sixth president's diplomacy furthered the cause of peace and good will, but it also sowed the seeds of distrust and hatred among certain "backward" nations. In the following excerpts Roosevelt discusses some of his principal ideas and policies concerning America's place in the world.

DIPLOMATIC NICETIES

. . . I take this opportunity to point out two or three matters to which I think the Department should pay heed in the future.[2]

In the first place, I wish to find out from the Department why it permitted the Chinese Ambassador today twice to use the phrase "Your Excellency" in addressing the President. Not only law but wise custom and propriety demand that the President shall be addrest only as "Mr. President" or as "The President." . . . Any title is silly when given the President. This title is rather unusually silly. But it is not only silly

---

[1] William H. Harbaugh, ed., *The Writings of Theodore Roosevelt* (Indianapolis and New York, 1967), p. xxxix.

[2] TR to the State Department, December 2, 1908. In Elting E. Morison and associates, eds., *The Letters of Theodore Roosevelt*, 8 vols. (Cambridge: Harvard University Press, 1951–54), VI, 1405–1406. Copyright 1951, 1952, 1954 by the President and Fellows of Harvard College. Reprinted by permission of the publisher.

but inexcusable for the State Department, which ought above all other Departments to be correct in its usage, to permit foreign representatives to fall into the blunder of using this title. I would like an immediate explanation of why the blunder was permitted and a statement in detail as to what has been done by the Department to prevent the commission of any similar blunder in the future.

Now, as to the address itself. I did not deliver it as handed me because it was fatuous and absurd. I have already had to correct the ridiculous telegram that was drafted for me to send to China on the occasion of the death of the Emperor and the Empress Dowager. I do not object to the utter fatuity of the ordinary addresses made to me by, and by me to, the representatives of foreign governments when they come to me to deliver their credentials or to say good-by. The occasion is merely formal and the absurd speeches interchanged are simply rather elaborate ways of saying good morning and good-by. . . .

But on a serious occasion, as in the present instance where a statesman of rank has come here on a mission which may possess real importance, then there should be some kind of effort to write a speech that shall be simple, and that shall say something, or, if this is deemed inexpedient, that shall at least not be of a fatuity so great that it is humiliating to read it. It should be reasonably grammatical, and should not be wholly meaningless. In the draft of the letter handed me, for instance, I am made to say of the letter I receive: "I accept it with quite exceptional sentiments as a message of especial friendship." Of course any boy in school who wrote a sentence like that would be severely and properly disciplined. The next sentence goes on: "I receive it with the more profound sentiments in that you bring it now no less from the Emperor." What in Heaven's name did the composer of this epistle mean by "more profound sentiments" and "quite exceptional sentiments"? Cannot he write ordinary English?

PANAMA

The control, in the interest of the commerce and traffic of the whole civilized world, of the means of undisturbed transit across the Isthmus of Panama has become of transcendent importance to the United States.[3] We have repeatedly exercised this control by intervening in the course of domestic dissension, and by protecting the territory from foreign invasion. . . .

The above recital of facts establishes beyond question: First, that the United States has for over half a century patiently and in good

[3] From the annual message to Congress, December 7, 1903. In James D. Richardson, ed., *A Compilation of the Messages and Papers of the Presidents, 1789–1904,* 10 vols. (New York: Bureau of National Literature and Art, 1904), X, 604–6.

faith carried out its obligations under the treaty of 1846; second, that when for the first time it became possible for Colombia to do anything in requital of the services thus repeatedly rendered to it for fifty-seven years by the United States, the Colombian Government peremptorily and offensively refused thus to do its part, even though to do so would have been to its advantage and immeasurably to the advantage of the State of Panama, at that time under its jurisdiction; third, that throughout this period revolutions, riots, and factional disturbances of every kind have occurred one after the other in almost uninterrupted succession, some of them lasting for months and even for years, while the central government was unable to put them down or to make peace with the rebels; fourth, that these disturbances instead of showing any sign of abating have tended to grow more numerous and more serious in the immediate past; fifth, that the control of Colombia over the Isthmus of Panama could not be maintained without the armed intervention and assistance of the United States. In other words, the Government of Colombia, though wholly unable to maintain order on the Isthmus, has nevertheless declined to ratify a treaty the conclusion of which opened the only chance to secure its own stability and to guarantee permanent peace on, and the construction of a canal across, the Isthmus.

Under such circumstances the Government of the United States would have been guilty of folly and weakness, amounting in their sum to a crime against the Nation, had it acted otherwise than it did when the revolution of November 3 last took place in Panama. This great enterprise of building the interoceanic canal can not be held up to gratify the whims, or out of respect to the governmental impotence, or to the even more sinister and evil political peculiarities, of people who, though they dwell afar off, yet, against the wish of the actual dwellers on the Isthmus, assert an unreal supremacy over the territory. The possession of a territory fraught with such peculiar capacities as the Isthmus in question carries with it obligations to mankind. The course of events has shown that this canal can not be built by private enterprise, or by any other nation than our own; therefore it must be built by the United States.

Every effort has been made by the Government of the United States to persuade Colombia to follow a course which was essentially not only to our interests and to the interests of the world, but to the interests of Colombia itself. These efforts have failed; and Colombia, by her persistence in repulsing the advances that have been made, has forced us, for the sake of our own honor, and of the interest and well-being, not merely of our own people, but of the people of the Isthmus of Panama and the people of the civilized countries of the world, to take decisive steps to bring to an end a condition of affairs which had become intolerable. The new Republic of Panama immediately offered to negotiate a treaty with us. This treaty I herewith submit. By it our interests are better safeguarded than in the treaty with Colombia which was ratified by the Senate at its last session. It is better in its terms than the treaties offered to us by the Republics of Nicaragua and Costa Rica. At last the right to begin this great undertaking is made available. Panama has done her part. All that remains is for the American Congress to do its part and forthwith this Republic will enter upon the execution of a project colossal in its size and of well-nigh incalculable possibilities for the good of this country and the nations of mankind.

*   *   *

I am interested in the Panama Canal because I started it.[4] If I had followed conventional, conservative methods, I should have submitted a dignified state paper of approximately two hundred pages to the Congress and the debate would have been going on yet, but I took the canal zone and let Congress debate, and while the debate goes on the canal does also.

THE ROOSEVELT COROLLARY

Through you I want to send my heartiest greetings to those gathered to celebrate the second anniversary of the Republic of Cuba.[5] I wish that it were possible to be present with you in person. I rejoice in what Cuba has done and especially in the way in which for the last two years her people have shown their desire and ability to accept in a serious spirit the responsibilities that accompany freedom. Such determination is vital, for those unable or unwilling to shoulder the responsibility of using their liberty aright can never in the long run preserve such liberty.

As for the United States, it must ever be a source of joy and gratification to good American citizens that they were enabled to play the part they did as regards Cuba. We freed Cuba from tyranny; we then stayed in the island until we had established civil order and laid the foundations for self-government and prosperity; we then made the island independent, and have since benefited her inhabitants by making closer the commercial relations between us. I hail what had been done in Cuba not merely for its own sake, but as showing the purpose and desire of this nation toward all the nations south of us. . . .

All that we desire is to see all neighboring countries stable, orderly and prosperous. Any country whose people conduct themselves well can count upon our hearty friendliness. . . . Brutal wrongdoing, or

[4] *New York Times,* March 24, 1911.
[5] TR to Elihu Root, May 20, 1904. In New York *Tribune,* May 21, 1904.

an impotence which results in a general loosening of the ties of civilized society, may finally require intervention by some civilized nation, and in the Western Hemisphere the United States cannot ignore this duty; but it remains true that our interests, and those of our southern neighbors, are in reality identical. All that we ask is that they shall govern themselves well, and be prosperous and orderly. Where this is the case they will find only helpfulness from us.

* * *

It is not true that the United States feels any land hunger or entertains any projects as regards the other nations of the western hemisphere save such as are for their welfare. . . .[6] If a nation shows that it knows how to act with reasonable efficiency and decency in social and political matters, if it keeps order and pays its obligations, it need fear no interference from the United States. Chronic wrongdoing, or an impotence which results in a general loosening of the ties of civilized society, may in America, as elsewhere, ultimately require intervention by some civilized nation, and in the western hemisphere the adherence of the United States to the Monroe Doctrine may force the United States, however reluctantly, in flagrant cases of such wrongdoing or impotence, to the exercise of an international police power. If every country washed by the Caribbean Sea would show the progress in stable and just civilization which with the aid of the Platt amendment Cuba has shown since our troops left the island, and which so many of the republics in both Americas are constantly and brilliantly showing, all question of interference by this nation with their affairs would be at an end.

THE ORIENT

Not only must we treat all nations fairly, but we must treat with justice and good-will all immigrants who come here under the law. . . .[7]

I am prompted to say this by the attitude of hostility here and there assumed toward the Japanese in this country. This hostility is sporadic and is limited to a very few places. Nevertheless, it is most discreditable to us as a people, and it may be fraught with the gravest consequences to the nation. . . . The Japanese have won in a single generation the right to stand abreast of the foremost and most enlightened peoples of Europe and America; they have won on their own merits and by

[6] From the annual message to Congress, December 6, 1904. In *Congressional Record*, 58th Cong., 3d sess., p. 19.

[7] From the annual message to Congress, December 4, 1906. In *Congressional Record*, 59th Congress, 2d sess., p. 31.

their own exertions the right to treatment on a basis of full and frank equality. . . .

Our nation fronts on the Pacific, just as it fronts on the Atlantic. We hope to play a constantly growing part in the great ocean of the Orient. We wish, as we ought to wish, for a great commercial development in our dealings with Asia; and it is out of the question that we should permanently have such development unless we freely and gladly extend to other nations the same measure of justice and good treatment which we expect to receive in return. It is only a very small body of our citizens that act badly. Where the Federal Government has power it will deal summarily with any such. Where the several States have power I earnestly ask that they also deal wisely and promptly with such conduct, or else this small body of wrong-doers may bring shame upon the great mass of their innocent and right-thinking fellows—that is, upon our nation as a whole. . . .

I recommend to the Congress that an act be passed specifically providing for the naturalization of Japanese who come here intending to become American citizens. One of the great embarrassments attending the performance of our international obligations is the fact that the statutes of the United States are entirely inadequate.

NAVAL PREPAREDNESS

In my own judgment the most important service that I rendered to peace was the voyage of the battle fleet round the world.[8] I had become convinced that for many reasons it was essential that we should have it clearly understood, by our own people especially, but also by other peoples, that the Pacific was as much our home waters as the Atlantic, and that our fleet could and would at will pass from one to the other of the two great oceans. It seemed to me evident that such a voyage would greatly benefit the navy itself; would arouse popular interest in and enthusiasm for the navy; and would make foreign nations accept as a matter of course that our fleet should from time to time be gathered in the Pacific, just as from time to time it was gathered in the Atlantic, and that its presence in one ocean was no more to be accepted as a mark of hostility to any Asiatic power than its presence in the Atlantic was to be accepted as a mark of hostility to any European power. I determined on the move without consulting the Cabinet, precisely as I took Panama without consulting the Cabinet. A council of war never fights, and in a crisis the duty of a leader is to lead and not to take refuge behind the generally timid

[8] Hermann Hagedorn, ed., *The Works of Theodore Roosevelt*, National Edition, 20 vols. (New York: Charles Scribner's Sons, 1926), XX, 535–37. Copyright 1913 by Charles Scribner's Sons. Reprinted by permission of the publisher.

wisdom of a multitude of councillors. At that time, as I happen to know, neither the English nor the German authorities believed it possible to take a fleet of great battleships around the world. They did not believe that their own fleets could perform the feat, and still less did they believe that the American fleet could. I made up my mind that it was time to have a show-down in the matter; because if it was really true that our fleet could not get from the Atlantic to the Pacific, it was much better to know it and be able to shape our policy in view of the knowledge. Many persons publicly and privately protested against the move on the ground that Japan would accept it as a threat. To this I answered nothing in public. In private I said that I did not believe Japan would so regard it because Japan knew my sincere friendship and admiration for her and realized that we could not as a nation have any intention of attacking her; and that if there were any such feeling on the part of Japan as was alleged that very fact rendered it imperative that that fleet should go. . . .

My prime purpose was to impress the American people; and this purpose was fully achieved. The cruise did make a very deep impression abroad; boasting about what we have done does not impress foreign nations at all, except unfavorably, but positive achievement does; and the two American achievements that really impressed foreign peoples during the first dozen years of this century were the digging of the Panama Canal and the cruise of the battle fleet round the world. But the impression made on our own people was of far greater consequence. No single thing in the history of the new United States navy has done as much to stimulate popular interest and belief in it as the world cruise.

INTERNATIONAL PEACE

We must ever bear in mind that the great end in view is righteousness, justice as between man and man, nation and nation, the chance to lead our lives on a somewhat higher level, with a broader spirit of brotherly good-will one for another.[9] Peace is generally good in itself, but it is never the highest good unless it comes as the handmaid of righteousness; and it becomes a very evil thing if it serves merely as a mask for cowardice and sloth, or as an instrument to further the ends of despotism or anarchy. . . .

The advance can be made along several lines. First of all, there can be treaties of arbitration. There are, of course, states so backward that a civilized community ought not to enter into an arbitration treaty

[9] From an address to the Nobel Prize Committee, delivered at Christiania, Norway, May 5, 1910. In Hagedorn, ed., *The Works of Theodore Roosevelt*, XVI, 306–9. Reprinted by permission of Charles Scribner's Sons.

with them, at least until we have gone much farther than at present in securing some kind of international police action. But all really civilized communities should have effective arbitration treaties among themselves. . . .

Secondly, there is the farther development of the Hague Tribunal, of the work of the conferences and courts at The Hague. . . . If I may venture the suggestion, it would be well for the statesmen of the world in planning for the erection of this world court, to study what has been done in the United States by the Supreme Court. I cannot help thinking that the Constitution of the United States, notably in the establishment of the Supreme Court and in the methods adopted for securing peace and good relations among and between the different States, offers certain valuable analogies to what should be striven for in order to secure, through The Hague courts and conferences, a species of world federation for international peace and justice. . . .

In the third place, something should be done as soon as possible to check the growth of armaments, especially vital armaments, by international agreement. No one power could or should act by itself; for it is eminently undesirable, from the standpoint of the peace of righteousness, that a power which really does believe in peace should place itself at the mercy of some rival which may at bottom have no such belief and no intention of acting on it. . . .

Finally, it would be a master stroke if those great powers honestly bent on peace would form a League of Peace, not only to keep the peace among themselves, but to prevent, by force if necessary, its being broken by others. The supreme difficulty in connection with developing the peace work of The Hague arises from the lack of any executive power, of any police power, to enforce the decrees of the court. . . . Each nation must keep well prepared to defend itself until the establishment of some form of international police power, competent and willing to prevent violence as between nations. As things are now, such power to command peace throughout the world could best be assured by some combination between those great nations which sincerely desire peace and have no thought themselves of committing aggressions.

8
The Progressive Movement

When he returned to the United States in 1910, after more than a year in Africa and Europe, Theodore Roosevelt was immediately drawn into the maelstrom of national politics. While campaigning for the Republican party and endeavoring to reconcile the warring factions that threatened to disrupt it, the former president enunciated a comprehensive program of his own which he called the "New Nationalism." During the next few years he elaborated this program and gave it forceful expression in his campaign for the presidency in 1912. Many of the reforms included in the New Nationalism of 1910–12 were proposals he had made to Congress in 1907 and 1908. Nevertheless, the New Nationalism embodied a synthesis of Roosevelt's maturing progressivism and the most forthright and advanced stage of his political reformism. The character of TR's progressivism is made clear in the documents that follow.

HOW I BECAME A PROGRESSIVE

I suppose I had a natural tendency to become a Progressive, anyhow.[1] That is, I was naturally a democrat, in believing in fair play for everybody. But I grew toward my present position, not so much as the result of study in the library or the reading of books—although I have been very much helped by such study and by such reading—as by actually living and working with men under many different conditions and seeing their needs from many different points of view.

The first set of our people with whom I associated so intimately as to get on thoroughly sympathetic terms with them were cow-punchers, then on the ranges in the West. I was so impressed with them that in doing them justice I did injustice to equally good citizens elsewhere whom I did not know; and it was a number of years before I grew to understand, first by associating with railway men, then with farmers, then with mechanics, and so on, that the things that I specially liked about my cow-puncher friends were, after all, to be found funda-

[1] TR, "How I Became a Progressive," *The Outlook,* CII (October 12, 1912), 294–95.

mentally in railway men, in farmers, in blacksmiths, carpenters—in fact, generally among my fellow American citizens.

Before I began to go with the cow-punchers, I had already, as the result of experience in the Legislature at Albany, begun rather timidly to strive for social and industrial justice. But at that time my attitude was that of giving justice from above. It was the experience on the range that first taught me to try to get justice for all of us by working on the same level with the rest of my fellow-citizens. . . .

For years I accepted the theory, as most of the rest of us then accepted it, that we already had popular government; that this was a government by the people. I believed the power of the boss was due only to the indifference and short-sightedness of the average decent citizen. Gradually it came over me that while this was half the truth, it was only half the truth, and that while the boss owed part of his power to the fact that the average man did not do his duty, yet that there was the further fact to be considered, that for the average man it had already been made very difficult instead of very easy for him to do his duty. I grew to feel a keen interest in the machinery for getting adequate and genuine popular rule, chiefly because I found that we could not get social and industrial justice without popular rule, and that it was immensely easier to get such popular rule by the means of machinery of the type of direct nominations at primaries, the short ballot, the initiative, referendum, and the like.

I usually found that my interest in any given side of a question of justice was aroused by some concrete case. It was the examination I made into the miseries attendant upon the manufacture of cigars in tenement-houses that first opened my eyes to the need of legislation on such subjects. My friends come from many walks of life. The need for a workmen's compensation act was driven home to me by my knowing a brakeman who had lost his legs in an accident, and whose family was thereby at once reduced from self-respecting comfort to conditions that at one time became very dreadful. Of course, after coming across various concrete instances of this kind, I would begin to read up on the subject, and then I would get in touch with social workers and others who were experts and could acquaint me with what was vital in the matter.

THE NEW NATIONALISM

. . . Our country—this great republic—means nothing unless it means the triumph of a real democracy, the triumph of popular government, and, in the long run, of an economic system under which each man shall be guaranteed the opportunity to show the best that there is in him.[2] That is why the history of America is now the central feature of the history of the world; for the world has set its face hopefully toward our democracy; and, O my fellow citizens, each one of you carries on your shoulders not only the burden of doing well for the sake of your own country, but the burden of doing well and of seeing that this nation does well for the sake of mankind.

There have been two great crises in our country's history: first, when it was formed, and then, again, when it was perpetuated; and, in the second of these great crises—in the time of stress and strain which culminated in the Civil War, on the outcome of which depended the justification of what had been done earlier. . . .

I do not speak of this struggle of the past merely from the historic standpoint. Our interest is primarily in the application to-day of the lessons taught by the contest of half a century ago. It is of little use for us to pay lip loyalty to the mighty men of the past unless we sincerely endeavor to apply to the problems of the present precisely the qualities which in other crises enabled the men of that day to meet those crises. . . .

Practical equality of opportunity for all citizens, when we achieve it, will have two great results. First, every man will have a fair chance to make of himself all that in him lies; to reach the highest point to which his capacities, unassisted by special privilege of his own and unhampered by the special privilege of others, can carry him, and to get for himself and his family substantially what he has earned. Second, equality of opportunity means that the commonwealth will get from every citizen the highest service of which he is capable. No man who carries the burden of the special privileges of another can give to the commonwealth that service to which it is fairly entitled.

I stand for the square deal. But when I say that I am for the square deal, I mean not merely that I stand for fair play under the present rules of the game, but that I stand for having those rules changed so as to work for a more substantial equality of opportunity and of reward for equally good service. . . .

Now, this means that our government, national and state, must be freed from the sinister influence or control of special interests. Exactly as the special interests of cotton and slavery threatened our political integrity before the Civil War, so now the great special business interests too often control and corrupt the men and methods of government for their own profit. We must drive the special interests out of politics. . . .

[2] From an address at Osawatomie, Kansas, August 31, 1910. In Theodore Roosevelt, *The New Nationalism*, with an Introduction and Notes by William E. Leuchtenburg (Englewood Cliffs, N.J.: Prentice-Hall, Inc., 1961), pp. 21–22, 24, 26–27, 30, 34–36. Copyright 1961 by Prentice-Hall, Inc. Reprinted by permission of the publisher.

The absence of effective state, and, especially, national, restraint upon unfair money-getting has tended to create a small class of enormously wealthy and economically powerful men, whose chief object is to hold and increase their power. The prime need is to change the conditions which enable these men to accumulate power which it is not for the general welfare that they should hold or exercise. We grudge no man a fortune which represents his own power and sagacity, when exercised with entire regard to the welfare of his fellows. . . .

. . . Let us admit also the right to regulate the terms and conditions of labor, which is the chief element of wealth, directly in the interest of the common good. The fundamental thing to do for every man is to give him a chance to reach a place in which he will make the greatest possible contribution to the public welfare. . . .

National efficiency has many factors. It is a necessary result of the principle of conservation widely applied. In the end it will determine our failure or success as a nation. National efficiency has to do, not only with natural resources and with men, but it is equally concerned with institutions. The state must be made efficient for the work which concerns only the people of the state; and the nation for that which concerns all the people. There must remain no neutral ground to serve as a refuge for lawbreakers, and especially for lawbreakers of great wealth, who can hire the vulpine legal cunning which will teach them how to avoid both jurisdictions. . . .

. . . The New Nationalism puts the national need before sectional or personal advantage. It is impatient of the utter confusion that results from local legislatures attempting to treat national issues as local issues. It is still more impatient of the impotence which springs from overdivision of governmental powers, the impotence which makes it possible for local selfishness or for legal cunning, hired by wealthy special interests, to bring national activities to a deadlock. This New Nationalism regards the executive power as the steward of the public welfare. It demands of the judiciary that it shall be interested primarily in human welfare rather than in property, just as it demands that the representative body shall represent all the people rather than any one class or section of the people.

A CONFESSION OF FAITH

To you, men and women who have come here to this great city of this great State formally to launch a new party, a party of the people of the whole Union, the National Progressive party, I extend my hearty greeting.[3] You are taking a bold and a greatly needed step for the

[3] From TR's address to the Progressive party national convention in Chicago, August 6, 1912. In *New York Times,* August 7, 1912.

service of our beloved country. The old parties are husks, with no real soul within either, divided on artificial lines, boss-ridden and privilege-controlled, each a jumble of incongruous elements, and neither daring to speak out wisely and fearlessly what should be said on the vital issues of the day. This new movement is a movement of truth, sincerity, and wisdom, a movement which proposes to put at the service of all our people the collective power of the people, through their governmental agencies, alike in the nation and in the several States. We propose boldly to face the real and great questions of the day, and not skilfully to evade them as do the old parties. We propose to raise aloft a standard to which all honest men can repair, and under which all can fight, no matter what their past political differences, if they are content to face the future and no longer to dwell among the dead issues of the past. We propose to put forth a platform which shall not be a platform of the ordinary and insincere kind, but shall be a contract with the people; and, if the people accept this contract by putting us in power, we shall hold ourselves under honorable obligation to fulfil every promise it contains as loyally as if it were actually enforceable under the penalties of the law.

The prime need to-day is to face the fact that we are now in the midst of a great economic evolution. There is urgent necessity of applying both common sense and the highest ethical standard to this movement for better economic conditions among the mass of our people if we are to make it one of healthy evolution and not one of revolution. . . .

The first essential in the Progressive programme is the right of the people to rule. . . .

I do not mean that we shall abandon representative government; on the contrary, I mean that we shall devise methods by which our government shall become really representative. To use such measures as the initiative, referendum, and recall indiscriminately and promiscuously on all kinds of occasions would undoubtedly cause disaster; but events have shown that at present our institutions are not representative—at any rate in many States, and sometimes in the nation—and that we cannot wisely afford to let this condition of things remain longer uncorrected. . . .

The American people, and not the courts, are to determine their own fundamental policies. The people should have power to deal with the effect of the acts of all their governmental agencies. This must be extended to include the effects of judicial acts as well as the acts of the executive and legislative representatives of the people. . . . I especially challenge the attention of the people to the need of dealing in far-reaching fashion with our human resources, and therefore our labor power. . . .

1. We hold that the public has a right to complete knowledge of the facts of work.

2. On the basis of these facts and with the recent discoveries of physicians and neurologists, engineers and economists, the public can formulate minimum occupational standards below which, demonstrably, work can be prosecuted only at a human deficit.

3. In the third place, we hold that all industrial conditions which fall below such standards should come within the scope of governmental action and control in the same way that subnormal sanitary conditions are subject to public regulation and for the same reason—because they threaten the general welfare. . . .

There is no body of our people whose interests are more inextricably interwoven with the interests of all the people than is the case with the farmers. The Country Life Commission should be revived with greatly increased powers; its abandonment was a severe blow to the interests of our people. . . .

Again and again while I was President, from 1902 to 1908, I pointed out that under the antitrust law alone it was neither possible to put a stop to business abuses nor possible to secure the highest efficiency in the service rendered by business to the general public. The antitrust law must be kept on our statute-books, and, as hereafter shown, must be rendered more effective in the cases where it is applied. . . .

. . . At the same time, a national industrial commission should be created which should have complete power to regulate and control all the great industrial concerns engaged in interstate business—which practically means all of them in this country. This commission should exercise over these industrial concerns like powers to those exercised over the railways by the Interstate Commerce Commission, and over the national banks by the comptroller of the currency, and additional powers if found necessary. . . .

Now, friends, this is my confession of faith. I have made it rather long because I wish you to know what my deepest convictions are on the great questions of to-day, so that if you choose to make me your standard-bearer in the fight you shall make your choice understanding exactly how I feel—and if, after hearing me, you think you ought to choose some one else, I shall loyally abide by your choice. The convictions to which I have come have not been arrived at as the result of study in the closet or the library, but from the knowledge I have gained through hard experience during the many years in which, under many and varied conditions, I have striven and toiled with men. I believe in a larger use of the governmental power to help remedy industrial wrongs, because it has been borne in on me by actual experience that without exercise of such power many of the wrongs will go unremedied. I believe in a larger opportunity for the people themselves directly to participate in government and to control their governmental agents, because long experience has taught me that without such control many of their agents will represent them badly. . . .

Surely there never was a fight better worth making than the one in which we are engaged. It little matters what befalls any one of us who for the time being stands in the forefront of the battle. I hope we shall win, and I believe that if we can wake the people to what the fight really means we shall win. But, win or lose, we shall not falter.

. . . Now to you men, who, in your turn, have come together to spend and be spent in the endless crusade against wrong, to you who face the future resolute and confident, to you who strive in a spirit of brotherhood for the betterment of our nation, to you who gird yourselves for this great new fight in the never-ending warfare for the good of humankind, I say in closing what in that speech I said in closing: We stand at Armageddon, and we battle for the Lord.

THE PROGRESSIVE PARTY AND THE NEGRO

. . . I believe that the Progressive Movement should be made from the beginning one in the interest of every honest, industrious, law-abiding colored man, just as it is in the interest of every honest, industrious, law-abiding white man.[4] I further believe that the surest way to render the movement impotent to help either the white man or the colored man in those regions of the South where the colored man is most numerous, would be to try to repeat the course that has been followed by the Republican Party in those districts for so many years, or to endeavor in the States in question to build up a Progressive Party by the same methods which in those States have resulted in making the Republican Party worse than impotent. . . .

The progress that has been made among the negroes of the South during these forty-five years has not been made as a result of political effort of the kind I have mentioned. It has been made as the result of effort along industrial and educational lines. Again allowing for the inevitable exception, it remains true, as one of the wisest leaders of the colored race has himself said, that the only white man who in the long run, can effectively help the colored man is that colored man's neighbor. There are innumerable white men in the South sincerely desirous of doing justice to the colored man, of helping him upward on his difficult path, of securing him just treatment before the law; white men who set their faces sternly against lynch law and mob violence, who attack all such abuses as peonage, who fight to keep

[4] TR to Julian La Rose Harris, August 1, 1912. In Elting E. Morison and associates, eds., *The Letters of Theodore Roosevelt*, 8 vols. (Cambridge: Harvard University Press, 1951–54), VII, 585, 588, 590. Copyright 1951, 1952, 1954 by the President and Fellows of Harvard College. Reprinted by permission of the publisher.

the school funds equitably divided between white and colored schools, who endeavor to help the colored man to become a self-supporting and useful member of the community. The white men who live elsewhere can best help the colored man in the South by upholding the hands of those white men of the South who are thus endeavoring to benefit and to act honestly by the colored men with whom they dwell in community neighborhood and with whose children their children will continue to dwell in community neighborhood. Actual experience for nearly half a century has shown that it is futile to endeavor to substitute for such action by the white man to his colored neighbor, action by outside white men, action which painful experience has shown to be impotent to help the colored man, but which does irritate the white man whom nevertheless it cannot control. . . .

We face certain actual facts, sad and unpleasant facts, but facts which must be faced if we are to dwell in the world of realities and not of shams, and if we are to try to make things better by deeds and not merely to delude ourselves by empty words. It would be much worse than useless to try to build up the Progressive Party in these Southern States where there is no real Republican Party, by appealing to the negroes or to the men who in the past have derived their sole standing from leading and manipulating the negroes. As a matter of fact and not of theory all that could possibly result from such action would be to create another impotent little corrupt faction of would-be officeholders, of delegates whose expenses to conventions had to be paid, and whose votes sometimes had to be bought. No real good could come from such action to any man, black or white; the negro would be hurt and not helped throughout the Union; the white man would be hurt in the South, the Progressive Party would be damaged irreparably at the beginning. I earnestly believe that by appealing to the best white men in the South, the men of justice and of vision as well as of strength and leadership, and by frankly putting the movement in their hands from the outset we shall create a situation by which the colored men of the South will ultimately get justice as it is not possible for them to get justice if we are to continue and perpetuate the present conditions.

9
The Politics of War and Peace

By the time of the mid-term elections of 1914, Roosevelt had begun to lose interest in domestic reform. He became increasingly hostile toward the Wilson administration and was particularly opposed to its conduct of foreign affairs. The war in Europe soon became almost an obsession with him, and he devoted himself with all of his characteristic energy to American preparedness and intervention. An impassioned patriot and extreme nationalist, TR remained until his death in 1919 one of the sharpest and most vocal critics of Woodrow Wilson's policies. The following selections are representative of Roosevelt's many articles and speeches and reveal the major ideas and concerns that preoccupied the colorful Colonel during these last years.

A TIMID AND SPIRITLESS NEUTRALITY

"Blessed are the peacemakers," not merely the peace-lovers; for action is what makes thought operative and valuable.[1] Above all, the peace-prattlers are in no way blessed. On the contrary, only mischief has sprung from the activities of the professional peace-prattlers, the ultrapacifists, who, with the shrill clamor of eunuchs, preach the gospel of the milk and water of virtue and the scream that belief in the efficacy of diluted moral mush is essential to salvation.

. . . I object to them, first, because they have proved themselves futile and impotent in working for peace, and, second, because they commit what is not merely the capital error but the crime against morality of failing to uphold righteousness as the all-important end toward which we should strive. In actual practice they advocate the peace of unrighteousness just as fervently as they advocate the peace of righteousness. . . .

I feel in the strongest way that we should have interfered, at least to the extent of the most emphatic diplomatic protest and at the very outset—and then by whatever further action was necessary—in regard

[1] From *America and the World War* (1915), in Hermann Hagedorn, ed., *The Works of Theodore Roosevelt*, National Edition, 20 vols. (New York: Charles Scribner's Sons, 1926), XVIII, 164, 166–67, 185. Copyright 1926 by Charles Scribner's Sons. Reprinted by permission of the publisher.

to the violation of the neutrality of Belgium; for this act was the earliest and the most important and, in its consequences the most ruinous of all the violations and offenses against treaties committed by any combatant during the war. . . .

If, instead of observing a timid and spiritless neutrality, we had lived up to our obligations by taking action in all of these cases without regard to which power it was that was alleged to have done wrong, we would have followed the only course that would both have told for world righteousness and have served our own self-respect. The course actually followed by Messrs. Wilson, Bryan, and Daniels has been to permit our own power for self-defense steadily to diminish while at the same time refusing to do what we were solemnly bound to do in order to protest against wrong and to render some kind of aid to weak nations that had been wronged. . . .

. . . The storm that is raging in Europe at this moment is terrible and evil; but it is also grand and noble. Untried men who live at ease will do well to remember that there is a certain sublimity even in Milton's defeated archangel, but none whatever in the spirits who kept neutral, who remained at peace, and dared side neither with hell nor with heaven. They will also do well to remember that when heroes have battled together, and have wrought good and evil, and when the time has come out of the contest to get all the good possible and to prevent as far as possible the evil from being made permanent, they will not be influenced much by the theory that soft and short-sighted outsiders have put themselves in better condition to stop war abroad by making themselves defenseless at home.

THE ELECTION OF 1916

In accordance with the message I sent to the Progressive National Convention as soon as I had received the notification that it had nominated me for President, I now communicate to you my reasons for declining the honor which I so deeply appreciate. . . .[2]

The results of the terrible world war of the last two years have now made it evident to all who are willing to see that in this country there must be spiritual and industrial preparedness along the lines of efficiency, of loyal service to the nation, and of practical application of the precept that each man must be his brother's keeper.

Furthermore, it is no less evident that this preparedness for the tasks of peace forms the only sound basis for that indispensable military preparedness which rests on universal military training and which finds expression in universal obligatory service in time of war.

[2] TR to the Progressive National Committee, June 22, 1916. In New York *Tribune*, June 27, 1916.

Such universal obligatory training and service are the necessary complements of universal suffrage and represent the realization of the true American, the democratic, ideal in both peace and war.

Sooner or later the national principles championed by the Progressives of 1912, must in their general effect be embodied in the structure of our national existence. With all my heart I shall continue to work for these great ideals, shoulder to shoulder with the men and women who in 1912 championed them. . . .

. . . The present Administration, during its three years of life, had been guilty of shortcomings more signal than those of any Administration since the days of Buchanan. . . .

Under these circumstances the Progressive National Committee at Chicago in January outlined our duty to seek common action with the Republican party. . . .

. . . We owe all of our present trouble with the professional German-American element in the United States to Mr. Wilson's timid and vacillating course during the last two years. . . .

The world is passing through a great crisis, and no man can tell what trial and jeopardy will have to be faced by this nation during the years immediately ahead. There is now no longer before us for decision the question as to what particular man we may severally most desire to see at the head of the government. We can decide only whether during these possibly vital years this country shall be intrusted to the leadership of Mr. Hughes or Mr. Wilson.

Mr. Wilson has been tried and found wanting. His party because of its devotion to the outworn theory of State rights, and because of its reliance upon purely sectional support, stands against the spirit of far-sighted nationalism which is essential if we are to deal adequately with our gravest social and industrial problems.

Mr. Wilson and his party have in actual practice lamentably failed to safeguard the interest and honor of the United States. They have brought us to impotence abroad and to division and weakness at home.

NATIONAL PREPAREDNESS

Preparedness must be of the soul no less than of the body.[3] We must keep lofty ideals steadily before us, and must train ourselves in practical fashion so that we may realize these ideals. Throughout our whole land we must have fundamental common purposes, to be achieved through education, through intelligent organization, and

[3] TR to S. Stanwood Menken, January 10, 1917. In Elting E. Morison and associates, eds., *The Letters of Theodore Roosevelt*, 8 vols. (Cambridge: Harvard University Press, 1951–54), VIII, 1144–47. Copyright 1951, 1952, 1954 by the President and Fellows of Harvard College. Reprinted by permission of the publisher.

through the recognition of the great vital standards of life and living. We must make Americanism and Americanization mean the same thing to the native born and to the foreign born; to the men and to the women; to the rich and to the poor; to the employer and to the wage-worker. . . .

Citizenship must mean an undivided loyalty to America; there can be no citizenship on the 50–50 basis; there can be no loyalty half to America and half to Germany, or England, or France, or Ireland, or any other country. Our citizens must be Americans, and nothing else, and if they try to be something else in addition, then they should be sent out of this country and back to the other country to which, in their hearts, they pay allegiance. We must have one American language; the language of the Declaration of Independence and the Constitution, of Lincoln's Gettysburg speech and Second Inaugural, and of Washington's farewell address. . . .

. . . I appeal to all Americans to join in the common effort for the common good. Any man who holds back, and refuses to serve his country with wholehearted devotion, on the ground that enough has not been done for him, will do well to remember that any such holding back, or lukewarmness of patriotism, is itself an admission of inferiority, an admission of personal unfitness for citizenship in a democracy, and ought to deprive him of the rights of citizenship. . . .

We need first and foremost a thoroughly efficient and large Navy; a navy kept under professional guidance; a navy trained at every point with the sole purpose of making it the most formidable possible instrument of war the moment that war comes; a navy, the mismanagement of which shall be treated as a capital offense against the nation. In the next place, we need a small but highly efficient regular army, of say a quarter million men. . . .

Side by side with this preparation of the manhood of the country must go the preparation of its resources. The Government should keep a record of every factory, or workshop, of any kind which would be called upon to render service in war, and of all the railroads. All the workers in such factories and railroads should be tabulated so that in the event of war they would not be sent to the front if they could do better service where they were—although as far as possible every strong man should be sent to the front, to the position of danger, while work done in safety should be done by women and old men. The transportation system should receive special study. . . .

Indeed, this military preparedness and the acceptance by the nation of the principle of universal, obligatory, military training in time of peace, as a basis of universal, obligatory service in time of war, would do more than anything else to help us solve our most pressing social and industrial problems in time of peace. It would Americanize and nationalize our people as nothing else could possibly do. It would teach our young men that there are other ideals besides making money. It would render them alert, energetic, self-reliant, capable of command, and willing to obey; respectful to others, and demanding respect from others for themselves. It would be the best possible way to teach us how to use our collective strength in order to accomplish those social and industrial tasks which must be done by all of us collectively if we are to do them well.

THE ROOSEVELT DIVISION

In view of the fact that Germany is now actually engaged in war with us, I again earnestly ask permission to be allowed to raise a division for immediate service at the front.[4] My purpose would be after some six weeks preliminary training here to take it direct to France for intensive training so that it could be sent to the front in the shortest possible time to whatever point was desired. I should of course ask no favors of any kind except that the division be put in the fighting line at the earliest possible moment. If the Department will allow me to assemble the division at Fort Sill, Oklahoma, and will give me what aid it can, and will furnish arms and supplies as it did for the early Plattsburg camps, I will raise the money to prepare the division until Congress can act, and we shall thereby gain a start of over a month in making ready. I would like to be authorized to raise three three-regiment brigades of infantry, one brigade of cavalry, one brigade of artillery, one regiment of engineers, one motorcycle machine-gun regiment, one aero squadron, and of course the supply branches, and so forth.

* * *

There is one point I did not have a chance to discuss with you, but I suppose it is hardly necessary.[5] If I were a younger man I would be entirely content to go in any position, as a second lieutenant, or as a private in the force. With my age I cannot do good service, however, unless as a general officer. I remember when I went to the Spanish War there was talk about rejecting me on account of my eyes; but, of course, even in the position I then went in, it was nonsense to reject me for any such reason. To the position which I now seek, of course,

[4] TR to Secretary of War Newton D. Baker (telegram), March 19, 1917. In Hagedorn, ed., *The Works of Theodore Roosevelt*, XIX, 190. Reprinted by permission of Charles Scribner's Sons.

[5] TR to Secretary Baker, April 12, 1917. In Hagedorn, ed., *The Works of Theodore Roosevelt*, XIX, 193. Reprinted by permission of Charles Scribner's Sons.

the physical examination does not apply, so long as I am fit to do the work, which I certainly can do—that is enlisting the best type of fighting men, and putting into them the spirit which will enable me to get the best possible results out of them in the actual fight. Hindenburg was, of course, a retired officer, who had been for years on the retired list, and who could not physically have passed an examination. I am not a Hindenburg; but I can raise and handle this division in a way that will do credit to the American people, and to you, and to the President.

THE GREAT ADVENTURE

Only those are fit to live who do not fear to die; and none are fit to die who have shrunk from the joy of life and the duty of life.[6] Both life and death are parts of the same Great Adventure. Never yet was worthy adventure worthily carried through by the man who put his personal safety first. Never yet was a country worth living in unless its sons and daughters were of that stern stuff which bade them die for it at need; and never yet was a country worth dying for unless its sons and daughters thought of life not as something concerned only with the selfish evanescence of the individual, but as a link in the great chain of creation and causation, so that each person is seen in his true relations as an essential part of the whole, whose life must be made to serve the larger and continuing life of the whole. Therefore it is that the man who is not willing to die, and the woman who is not willing to send her man to die, in a war for a great cause, are not worthy to live. Therefore it is that the man and woman who in peace-time fear or ignore the primary and vital duties and the high happiness of family life, who dare not beget and bear and rear the life that is to last when they are in their graves, have broken the chain of creation, and have shown that they are unfit for companionship with the souls ready for the Great Adventure. . . .

With all my heart I believe in the joy of living; but those who achieve it do not seek it as an end in itself, but as a seized and prized incident of hard work well done and of risk and danger never wantonly courted, but never shirked when duty commands that they be faced. And those who have earned joy, but are rewarded only with sorrow, must learn the stern comfort dear to great souls, the comfort that springs from the knowledge taught in times of iron that the law of worthy living is not fulfilled by pleasure, but by service, and by sacrifice when only thereby can service be rendered.

[6] From *The Great Adventure: Present-Day Studies in American Nationalism* (1918), in Hagedorn, ed., *The Works of Theodore Roosevelt*, XIX, 243–44. Reprinted by permission of Charles Scribner's Sons.

UNCONDITIONAL SURRENDER

When the American people speak for unconditional surrender, it means that Germany must accept whatever terms the United States and its allies think necessary in order to right the dreadful wrongs that have been committed and to safeguard the world for at least a generation to come from another attempt by Germany to secure world dominion.[7] Unconditional surrender is the reverse of a negotiated peace. The interchange of notes, which has been going on between our government and the governments of Germany and Austria during the last three weeks, means, of course, if persisted in, a negotiated peace. . . .

Those of us who believe in unconditional surrender regard Germany's behavior during the last five years as having made her the outlaw among nations. In private life sensible men and women do not negotiate with an outlaw or grow sentimental about him, or ask for a peace with him on terms of equality if he will give up his booty. . . .

We ought to treat Germany in precisely this manner. It is a sad and dreadful thing to have to face some months or a year or so of additional bloodshed, but it is a much worse thing to quit now and have the children now growing up obliged to do the job all over again, with ten times as much bloodshed and suffering, when their turn comes. The surest way to secure a peace as lasting as that which followed the downfall of Napoleon is to overthrow the Prussianized Germany of the Hohenzollerns as Napoleon was overthrown. If we enter into a league of peace with Germany and her vassal allies, we must expect them to treat the arrangement as a scrap of paper whenever it becomes to their interest to do so.

PRESIDENT WILSON AND THE PEACE CONFERENCE

No public end of any kind will be served by President Wilson's going with Mr. Creel, Mr. House, and his other personal friends to the Peace Conference. . . .[8]

Ten days before election Mr. Wilson issued an appeal to the American people in which he frankly abandoned the position of President of the whole people; assumed the position, not merely of party leader, but of party dictator, and appealed to the voters as such. Most of Mr.

[7] Kansas City, Mo., *Star*, October 26, 1918. Reprinted by permission of the Kansas City *Star*.

[8] Kansas City, Mo., *Star*, November 26, 1918. Reprinted by permission of the Kansas City *Star*.

Wilson's utterances on public questions have been susceptible to at least two conflicting interpretations. But on this question he made the issue absolutely clear. He asked that the people return a Democratic majority. . . . His appeal was not merely against any Republican being elected, but against any Democrat who wished to retain his conscience in his own keeping. . . .

The issue was perfectly, clearly drawn. The Republican party was prowar and anti-Administration, the Democratic party was officially pro-Administration without any mind or conscience of its own and prowar or antiwar according to the way in which Mr. Wilson changed his mind overnight or between dawn and sunset. The Americans refused to sustain Mr. Wilson. They elected a heavily Republican house and to the surprise of every one carried a majority in the Senate. On Mr. Wilson's own say-so they repudiated his leadership. . . .

Under these circumstances our allies and our enemies, and Mr. Wilson himself, should all understand that Mr. Wilson has no authority whatever to speak for the American people at this time. His leadership has just been emphatically repudiated by them. The newly elected Congress comes far nearer than Mr. Wilson to having a right to speak the purposes of the American people at this moment. Mr. Wilson and his fourteen points and his four supplementary points and his five complementary points and all his utterances every which way have ceased to have any shadow of right to be accepted as expressive of the will of the American people. He is President of the United States, he is part of the treaty-making power, but he is only part. . . . If he will in good faith act in this way all good citizens in good faith will support him, just as they will support the Senate under similar circumstances.

But there isn't the slightest indication that he intends so to act. The most striking manifestation of his purpose is that he sent over Mr. Creel and sixteen of his employees who are officially announced as "the United States official press mission to the Peace Conference," and, with more self-satisfaction, the committee announces, "to interpret the work of the Peace Conference by keeping up world-wide propaganda to disseminate American accomplishments and American ideals." . . .

This is a very grave offense against our own people, but it may be a worse offense against both our allies and ourselves. America played in the closing months of the war a gallant part, but not in any way the leading part, and she played this part only by acting in strictest agreement with our allies and under the joint high command. She should take precisely the same attitude at the Peace Conference. . . .

It is our business to act with our allies and to show an undivided front with them against any move of our late enemies. I am no Utopian. I understand entirely that there can be shifting alliances, I understand entirely that twenty years hence or thirty years hence we don't know what combinations we may have to face, and for this reason I wish to see us preparing our own strength in advance and trust to nothing but our own strength for our own self-defense as our permanent policy. But in the present war we have won only by standing shoulder to shoulder with our allies and presenting an undivided front to the enemy. It is our business to show the same loyalty and good faith at the Peace Conference.

PART TWO

ROOSEVELT VIEWED BY HIS CONTEMPORARIES

A perceptive New York politician, describing one of Theodore Roosevelt's campaign appearances during the gubernatorial race of 1898, noted the telling impact the Rough Rider's very appearance and personality had upon his audience: "He spoke about ten minutes—the speech was nothing, but the man's presence was everything. It was electrical, magnetic. I looked in the faces of hundreds and saw only pleasure and satisfaction. When the train moved away, scores of men and women ran after the train, waving hats and handkerchiefs and cheering, trying to keep him in sight as long as possible." [1] In successfully dramatizing himself and his policies, Roosevelt gave a classic demonstration of how a democratic leader can use public opinion to advance his causes. But he did more than that. By capturing the imagination of his fellow citizens, he became a many-faceted symbol to his contemporaries, a symbol that embodied much of the national character. The selections in this part of the book suggest the strong impression TR's leadership made on the Americans of his day and the most compelling images he stimulated in the American mind. They also include some illuminating observations on aspects of the twenty-sixth president's personality and politics by people who knew him well.

10

Civic Reformer

Despite his genteel background and conservative inclinations, Roosevelt was identified as a political reformer from the very beginning of his public career. He became known as a

[1] William T. O'Neil to J. S. Van Duzer, November 1, 1898. Quoted in Elting E. Morison and associates, eds., *The Letters of Theodore Roosevelt*, 8 vols. (Cambridge, 1951–54), II, 885.

*force for righteousness in public life and as a powerful advocate
of such fundamentals as honesty in government, opposition to
the spoils system, and the duty of the citizen to strengthen the
moral basis of politics. This symbolism is evident in the documents that follow.*

JOE MURRAY

After his nomination Theodore Roosevelt, [Jacob] Hess, [Wil-
lard] Bullard, and I went out on a personal canvass.[2] It was the custom in those days to visit the gin-mills, the stores, and places of business. The first place we happened to go into was the lager-beer saloon
on Sixth Avenue, near Fifty-fifth Street kept by a German named
Fischer. Hess introduced Mr. Roosevelt to the proprietor as the candidate for Assembly. Mr. Fischer says to him: "Well, Mr. Roosevelt,
the liquor interest has not been getting a square deal. We are paying
excessive taxes. I have no doubt that you will try to give us some relief
when you get up to the Legislature." (One of the grievances of Mr.
Fischer was that the license was too high.) Mr. Roosevelt asked him:
"Mr. Fischer, what is the license now?" Mr. Fischer named the figure
—what he had to pay—and Mr. Roosevelt says, "Well, that's not right.
I don't think you pay enough. I thought it would be at least twice as
much!"
After that we hustled him out and told him that he had better see
to the college boys and his friends on Fifth Avenue, the society folks;
that Hess, Bullard, and I would do the other end.

NEW YORK TIMES

Mr. Roosevelt has a most refreshing habit of calling men and
things by their right names, and in these days of judicial, ecclesiastical,
and journalistic subserviency to the robber-barons of the Street, it
needs some little courage in any public man to characterize them and
their acts in fitting terms.[3] There is a splendid career open for a young
man of position, character, and independence like Mr. Roosevelt who

[2] Lawrence F. Abbott, *Impressions of Theodore Roosevelt* (Garden City: Doubleday, Page & Company, 1920), 41. Copyright 1919 by Doubleday, Page & Company.
Reprinted by permission of Laura Abbott Dale. Murray was a minor Republican
leader who had a hand in Roosevelt's nomination for the New York State
Assembly in 1881.

[3] Undated editorial (1882). Quoted in Joseph Bucklin Bishop, *Theodore Roosevelt
and His Time Shown in His Own Letters*, 2 vols. (New York: Charles Scribner's
Sons, 1920), I, 12. Copyright 1920 by Charles Scribner's Sons; copyright renewed
1948 by Joseph Bucklin Bishop. Reprinted by permission of the publisher.

can denounce the legalized robbery of Gould and his allies without descending to the turgid abuse of the demagogue, and without being restrained by the cowardly caution of the politician.

JACOB A. RIIS

. . . It could not have been long after I wrote "How the Other Half Lives" that he came to the *Evening Sun* office one day looking for me.[4] I was out, and he left his card, merely writing on the back of it that he had read my book and had "come to help." That was all and it tells the whole story of the man. I loved him from the day I first saw him; nor ever in all the years that have passed has he failed of the promise made then. No one ever helped as he did. . . .

. . . There is very little ease where Theodore Roosevelt leads, as we all of us found out. The lawbreaker found it out who predicted scornfully that he would "knuckle down to politics the way they all did," and lived to respect him, though he swore at him, as the one of them all who was stronger than pull. The peace-loving citizen who hastened to Police Headquarters with anxious entreaties to "use discretion" in the enforcement of unpopular laws found it out and went away with a new and breathless notion welling up in him of an official's sworn duty. . . .

. . . It is long since I have enjoyed anything so much as I did those patrol trips of ours on the "last tour" between midnight and sunrise, which earned for him the name of Haroun al Roosevelt. I had at last found one who was willing to get up when other people slept—including, too often, the police—and see what the town looked like then. He was more than willing. I laid out the route, covering ten or a dozen patrol-posts, and we met at 2 A.M. on the steps of the Union League Club, objects of suspicion on the part of two or three attendants and a watchman who shadowed us as night-prowlers till we were out of their bailiwick. I shall never forget that first morning when we travelled for three hours along First and Second and Third avenues, from Forty-second Street to Bellevue, and found of ten patrolmen just one doing his work faithfully. Two or three were chatting on saloon corners and guyed the President of the Board when he asked them if that was what they were there for. One was sitting asleep on a butter-tub in the middle of the sidewalk, snoring so that you could hear him across the street, and was inclined to be "sassy" when aroused and told to go about his duty. Mr. Roosevelt was a most energetic roundsman and a fair one to boot. It was that quality which speedily won him the affection of the force. . . .

[4] Jacob A. Riis, *The Making of an American* (New York, 1901), pp. 327–28, 330, 332–33.

Looking after his patrolmen was not the only errand that took him abroad at night. As Police President, Mr. Roosevelt was a member of the Health Board, and sometimes it was the tenements we went inspecting when the tenants slept. He was after facts, and learned speedily to get them as he could. When, as Governor, he wanted to know just how the Factory Law was being executed, he came down from Albany and spent a whole day with me personally investigating tenements in which sweating was carried on. I had not found a Governor before, or a Police President either, who would do it; but so he learned exactly what he wanted to know, and what he ought to do, and did it.

I never saw Theodore Roosevelt to better advantage than when he confronted the labor men at their meeting-place, Clarendon Hall. The police were all the time having trouble with strikers and their "pickets." Roosevelt saw that it was because neither party understood fully the position of the other and, with his usual directness, sent word to the labor organizations that he would like to talk it over with them. At his request I went with him to the meeting. It developed almost immediately that the labor men had taken a wrong measure of the man. They met him as a politician playing for points, and hinted at trouble unless their demands were met. Mr. Roosevelt broke them off short:—

"Gentlemen!" he said, with that snap of the jaws that always made people listen, "I asked to meet you, hoping that we might come to understand one another. Remember, please, before we go farther, that the worst injury any one of you can do to the cause of labor is to counsel violence. It will also be worse for himself. Understand distinctly that order will be kept. The police will keep it. Now we can proceed."

I was never so proud and pleased as when they applauded him to the echo.

WILLIAM ALLEN WHITE

. . . I met Theodore Roosevelt.[5] He sounded in my heart the first trumpet call of the new time that was to be. I went hurrying home from our first casual meeting, in the office of an assistant of the Navy Department, to tell Sallie of the marvel of the meeting. I was afire with the splendor of the personality that I had met, and I walked up and down our little bedroom at the Normandie trying to impart to her some of the marvel that I saw in this young man. We were to lunch

[5] *The Autobiography of William Allen White* (New York: The Macmillan Co., 1946), pp. 297–99. Copyright 1946 by the Macmillan Company. Reprinted by permission of the publisher.

together the next day at the Army and Navy Club, where I went stepping on air, as one goes to meet an apparition. It was a rather somber old barn in those days, that club, and we sat there for an hour after lunch and talked our jaws loose about everything. I had never known such a man as he, and never shall again. He overcame me. And in the hour or two we spent that day at lunch, and in a walk down F Street he poured into my heart such visions, such ideals, such hopes, such a new attitude toward life and patriotism and the meaning of things, as I had never dreamed men had. We had this in common: neither of us could work up any enthusiasm for McKinley. I remember the first shock of pain with which he revealed not only his scorn for McKinley and his kind, but his disgust with the plutocracy that Hanna was establishing in the land. For Hanna, he had a certain large, joyous tolerance as a man, but for the government he was maintaining, for the reign of privilege he was constructing, for the whole deep and damnable alliance between business and politics for the good of business, Roosevelt was full of vocal eloquence and ironic rage. That was the order which I had upheld, to which I was committed, to which I had commended my soul. Yet so strong was this young Roosevelt—hard-muscled, hard-voiced even when the voice cracked in falsetto, with hard, wriggling jaw muscles, and snapping teeth, even when he cackled in raucous glee, so completely did the personality of this man overcome me that I made no protest and accepted his dictum as my creed. Presently we launched out into Heaven knows what seas of speculation, what excursions of delight, into books and men and manners, poetry and philosophy—"cabbages and kings!" After that I was his man.

It was not the ten years between us. It was more than the background of his achievements in politics. It was something besides his social status which itself might have influenced me in those days, something greater even than his erudition and his cultural equipment, that overcame me. It was out of the spirit of the man, the undefinable equation of his identity, body, mind, emotion, the soul of him, that grappled with me and, quite apart from reason, brought me into his train. It was youth and the new order calling youth away from the old order. It was the inexorable coming of change into life, the passing of the old into the new. . . .

Theodore Roosevelt and I, walking that summer day under the elms on F Street in Washington, going from the lunch at the Army and Navy Club, visioned a vast amount of justice to come in the cruel world. . . .

A few months later he sent me his book "American Ideals and Other Essays." I read it with feelings of mingled astonishment and trepidation. It shook my foundations, for it questioned things as they are. It challenged a complacent plutocracy. I did not dream that anyone, save the fly-by-night demagogues of Populism, had any question about the divine right of the well-to-do to rule the world. But that book was filled with an unsettling arraignment of the more predatory representatives of our American plutocracy. As a defender of the faith, I had met my first heretic.

11
Outdoorsman

Theodore Roosevelt's fascination with the outdoors was evident in the titles of his books, which included Ranch Life and the Hunting Trail, The Wilderness Hunter, *and* African Game Trails. *His delight in physical activity and outdoor exertion—in "the strenuous life"—caught the fancy of the American people. Almost from the beginning of his political career, Roosevelt was identified in the public mind with the great outdoors and the receding frontier. His colorful experiences as cowboy, hunter, naturalist, and westerner, which he himself described in great detail, seemed to have enormous appeal to a people who were already becoming nostalgic over the passing of the cattle kingdom, the disappearance of the wilderness, and the decline of rural life. In any case, one of the symbols TR projected to his contemporaries was that of the ardent outdoorsman.*

A WESTERN NEWSPAPER IN 1885

Rugged, bronzed, and in the prime of health, Theodore Roosevelt passed through St. Paul yesterday returning from his Dakota ranch to New York and civilization.[1] There was very little of the whilom dude in his rough and easy costume, with a large handkerchief tied loosely about his neck; but the eyeglasses and the flashing eyes behind them, the pleasant smile and the hearty grasp of hand remained. There was the same eagerness to hear from the world of politics, and the same frank willingness to answer all questions propounded. The slow, exasperating drawl and the unique accent that the New Yorker feels he must use when visiting a less blessed portion of civilization have disappeared, and in their place is a nervous, energetic manner of talking with the flat accent of the West. Roosevelt is changed from the New York club man to the thorough Westerner, but the change is only in surface indications, and he is the same thoroughly good fellow he has always been.

[1] Undated article from the St. Paul *Pioneer Press.* Quoted in Hermann Hagedorn, *Roosevelt in the Bad Lands* (Boston: Houghton Mifflin Company, 1921), p. 308. Copyright 1921 by Houghton Mifflin Company. Reprinted by permission of the publisher.

JOHN BURROUGHS

From his ranch days in Montana to the past year or two, I saw and was with Roosevelt many times and in many places.[2] In Yellowstone Park in the spring of 1903, in his retreat in the woods of Virginia during the last term of his presidency, at Oyster Bay at various times, in Washington at the White House, and at my place on the Hudson, I have felt the arousing and stimulating impact of his wonderful personality. When he came into the room it was as if a strong wind had blown the door open. You felt his radiant energy before he got halfway up the stairs.

When we went birding together it was ostensibly as teacher and pupil, but it often turned out that the teacher got as many lessons as he gave.

Early in May, during the last term of his presidency, he asked me to go with him to his retreat in the woods of Virginia, called "Pine Knot," and help him name his birds. Together we identified more than seventy-five species of birds and wild fowl. He knew them all but two, and I knew them all but two. He taught me Bewick's wren and one of the rare warblers, and I taught him the swamp sparrow and the pine warbler. A few days before he had seen Lincoln's sparrow in the old weedy field. On Sunday, after church, he took me there and we loitered around for an hour, but the sparrow did not appear. Had he found this bird again, he would have had one ahead of me. The one subject I do know, and ought to know, is the birds. It has been one of the main studies of a long life. He knew the subject as well as I did, while he knew with the same thoroughness scores of other subjects of which I am entirely ignorant.

He was a naturalist on the broadest grounds, uniting much technical knowledge of the daily lives and habits of all forms of wild life. He probably knew tenfold more natural history than all the presidents who had preceded him, and, I think one is safe in saying, more human history also.

In Yellowstone Park when I was with him, he carried no gun, but one day as we were riding along, he saw a live mouse on the ground beside the road. He instantly jumped out of the sleigh and caught the mouse in his hands; and that afternoon he skinned it in the approved taxidermist's way, and sent it to the United States Museum in Washington. It proved to be a species new to the Park.

In looking over the many letters I have had from him, first and last, I find that the greater number of them are taken up with the discus-

[2] Burroughs, "Theodore Roosevelt," *Natural History*, XIX (January, 1919), 5–7. Reprinted by permission of *Natural History*.

sion of natural history problems, such as Darwin's theory of natural selection, "sports," protective coloring. He would not allow himself, nor would he permit others to dogmatize about nature. He knew how infinitely various are her moods and ways, and not infrequently did he take me to task for being too sweeping in my statements.

When, in the early part of the last decade, while he was President, there was a serious outbreak of nature-faking in books and in various weekly and monthly periodicals, Roosevelt joined me and others in a crusade against the fakers and wielded the "big stick" with deadly effect. He detected a sham naturalist as quickly as he did a trading politician.

GEORGE BIRD GRINNELL

Roosevelt called often at my office to discuss the broad country that we both loved, and we came to know each other extremely well.[3] Though chiefly interested in big game and its hunting, and telling interestingly of events that had occurred on his own hunting trips, Roosevelt enjoyed hearing of the birds, the small mammals, the Indians, and the incidents of travel of early expeditions on which I had gone. He was always fond of natural history, having begun, as so many boys have done, with birds; but as he saw more and more of outdoor life his interest in the subject broadened and later it became a passion with him.

Besides these subjects we had this in common, that we were both familiar with life on a cow-ranch, and that the glamour of the cowboy's life—which to those who had only read of it seemed so romantic —had quite worn off, and we knew this life for what it was—the hardest kind of work. . . .

It was somewhat later than this, perhaps in the autumn of 1887, that Roosevelt suggested the establishment of a club of amateur riflemen, an organization which should be made up of good sportsmen who were also good big-game hunters. The project seemed one that might do good, and he became enthusiastic about it, and in December, 1887, invited a dozen men to dine with him at his house on Madison Avenue, and there proposed the formation of the club. Of the men present at that dinner only three are now living.

The club, named for Boone and for Crockett, was founded in December, 1887, and Roosevelt became the first president. The purposes, as expressed in the constitution, show fairly well the attitude of

[3] Grinnell, "Introduction," in Hermann Hagedorn, ed., *The Works of Theodore Roosevelt*, National Edition, 20 vols. (New York: Charles Scribner's Sons, 1926), I, xv–xvii, xix. Copyright 1926 by Charles Scribner's Sons. Reprinted by permission of the publisher.

the more advanced sportsmen of the time. These purposes were to promote (1) manly sport with the rifle, (2) travel and exploration in this country, (3) the preservation of our large game, (4) inquiry into and the recording of observations on the natural history of wild animals, and (5) to bring about interchange of opinions and ideas on hunting, travel, and exploration in game localities. . . .

When Roosevelt went into the West, inhabitants there were few. The old-time independent spirit still prevailed, and one man was just as good as another. . . . Roosevelt recognized this attitude of mind—which at first must have astonished him, as it did other Eastern men of the time—and he described it entertainingly in one or two of his Western books. He sympathized with the independent spirit and adjusted himself at once to the situations which it constantly brought up.

12
Man of Letters

For a period of several years in the 1880s and 1890s Roosevelt's literary output was so great that he could accurately be termed a professional man of letters. As he became increasingly involved in politics in the late nineties, he found less and less time to devote to writing. Yet he continued throughout his life to write essays and books, in addition to a vast number of letters, and to reveal an extraordinary interest in the literary world. "No American President," remarks William H. Harbaugh, "was so widely, and in certain areas, so deeply read as he. No President enjoyed literature more, wrote history as well, or understood nature better." [1] The following selection by one of the editors of The Outlook *evaluates TR as a writer and suggests some of the attributes that revealed him as a many-sided man.*

The first thing that strikes the ordinary observer about Roosevelt's work as a man of letters is its prodigious volume.[2] The list of books which he published—exclusive of pamphlets, occasional addresses, and uncollected magazine articles—numbers at least thirty separate titles. . . .

One of his official secretaries has said that, during his governorship and Presidency, Roosevelt wrote one hundred and fifty thousand letters. . . .

. . . If the estimate that Roosevelt produced eighteen millions of written words in his lifetime is at all reasonable, that alone would represent the work of thirty years of the lifetime of a literary man. . . .

. . . The very fact that he was so profuse in his writing makes some of it diffuse. It varies very much in merit, but it must be remembered that he did not have the leisure for incubation, consideration, and revision which the professional man of letters requires. Most of his writing was done at high pressure or in extraordinary circumstances. Father Zahm, the well-known scientist and man of letters in the Cath-

[1] William H. Harbaugh, ed., *The Writings of Theodore Roosevelt* (Indianapolis and New York, 1967), p. xviii.

[2] Lawrence F. Abbott, *Impressions of Theodore Roosevelt* (Garden City: Doubleday, Page & Company, 1920), pp. 169–72, 183–85, 196–97. Copyright 1919 by Doubleday, Page & Company. Reprinted by permission of Laura Abbott Dale.

olic Church—who accompanied Roosevelt on a large part of his South American explorations, and who originally proposed that trip—thus describes his two methods of work, in an article published in the *Outlook* not long after Roosevelt's death:

> The articles intended for one of the magazines of which he was a contributor were dictated to his secretary, and dictated for the most part immediately after the occurrence of the events described, while all of the facts were still fresh in his memory. Descriptions of scenery were rarely delayed more than one day, usually not more than a few hours. As soon as he returned from a visit to a museum, a cattle ranch, or a public gathering of any kind he called his secretary, and we soon heard the clicking of the keys of the typewriter. And it mattered not where he happened to be at the time—on a railway train, or on a steamer, or in a hotel—it was all the same. The work had to be done, and it was accomplished at the earliest possible moment. . . .
>
> The articles which appeared in another magazine describing his hunting experiences in Matto Grosso, unlike those recounting incidents of his triumphal march through other parts of South America, were written by his own hand, and often with the expenditure of great labour. Most people have come to believe that because Roosevelt wrote so much—and that often under the most unfavourable conditions—he must therefore have dashed off his articles for the press with little or no effort. Nothing is further from the truth. No one was more painstaking or conscientious than Roosevelt was in his literary work. . . .

He was a voracious and omnivorous reader. It is impossible to estimate the amount of Roosevelt's reading but it must have been phenomenally large for he read all sorts of books, modern and ancient, at all sorts of times and with almost unbelievable rapidity. . . .

Roosevelt had this gift in reading. The child laboriously reads syllable by syllable or word by word; the practised adult reads line by line; Roosevelt read almost page by page and yet remembered what he read. . . .

He read while waiting for trains and for people to keep appointments and when driving in his automobile to the city. I have seen him pick up a book surrounded by a roomful of talking and laughing friends and in a moment become so absorbed in it that he had no more knowledge of what was going on about him than if he had been in a cloister cell. During the railway journey from Khartum to Cairo on the tour of 1910, described more fully in a later chapter, a special dinner was to be served one evening in the private saloon dining car placed at Roosevelt's disposal by the Governor-General of the Sudan. This dinner was to be attended by some important officials and other guests, who had taken the train at one of the stations we passed through and were to leave it at another specified stopping-place. It was therefore essential that the company should assemble at the table promptly, but when dinner was announced Mr. Roosevelt was nowhere to be found. I searched the train for him and finally discovered him in one of the white enamelled lavatories with its door half open where, standing under an electric light, he was busily engaged in reading, while he braced himself in the angle of the two walls against the swaying motion of the train, oblivious to time and surroundings. The book in which he was absorbed was Lecky's "History of Rationalism in Europe." He had chosen this peculiar reading room both because the white enamel reflected a brilliant light and he was pretty sure of uninterrupted quiet. . . .

. . . He had a deep love for pure beauty in literature. Keats's "Ode on a Grecian Urn" was, for example, one of his favourite poems. Its appeal to him was, I think, not merely because of its music and the artistry of its form, but because it takes its reader completely out of material life and puts him into the quieting and problemless universe of pure imagination.

13
Strong President

It was Roosevelt's leadership during the years of his presidency, of course, that exerted the most influence upon the thinking of his contemporaries and established the basis for his historical reputation as a significant figure in twentieth-century American politics. The selections that follow illuminate the impact of Roosevelt's presidency upon his generation and the reasons many Americans considered him a great chief executive.

CAMPAIGNER

[In 1900] Roosevelt took his full share in campaigning for the Republican ticket.[1] He spoke in the East and in the West, and for the first time the people of many of the States heard him speak and saw his actual presence. His attitude as a speaker, his gestures, the way in which his pent-up thoughts seemed almost to strangle him before he could utter them, his smile showing the white rows of teeth, his fist clenched as if to strike an invisible adversary, the sudden dropping of his voice, and leveling of his forefinger as he became almost conversational in tone, and seemed to address special individuals in the crowd before him, the strokes of sarcasm, stern and cutting, and the swift flashes of humor which set the great multitude in a roar, became in that summer and autumn familiar to millions of his countrymen; and the cartoonists made his features and gestures familiar to many other millions.

* * *

Col. Roosevelt was also forceful as an orator and campaigner.[2] He violated all the canons of oratory, but was successful in spite of his voice and manner. In the end he capitalized even his defects, and learned how to make the most telling use of the falsetto in his voice,

[1] William Roscoe Thayer, *Theodore Roosevelt: An Intimate Biography* (Boston: Houghton Mifflin Company, 1919), p. 151. Copyright 1919 by the Houghton Mifflin Company. Reprinted by permission of the publisher.

[2] Charles Edward Merriam, *Four American Party Leaders: Henry Ward Beecher Foundation Lectures Delivered at Amherst College* (New York: The Macmillan Company, 1926), pp. 38–39. If there is a known address for the estate of Charles Edward Merriam, please notify Prentice-Hall, Inc., Englewood Cliffs, New Jersey.

of his well known teeth, and of his pile-driver manner. Not endowed with a golden voice or graceful manner or master of marvelous rhetoric as some have been, he was nevertheless one of the most effective speakers of his time—perhaps the most effective, if the test is that of winning votes and support. He made an impression of great sincerity, great energy and determination, and solid practical judgment. Neither brilliance nor its shadow rashness appeared in him, but the substantial qualities of a sturdy Dutch statesman with a dash of *élan*.

He was also a master in the art of publicity from the earliest days. His material was prepared well in advance for the press, and the reporters were never left stranded for copy, or for lack of an adroit interview. Perhaps better than any of his contemporaries he understood the value of sustained and favorable newspaper comment. He knew when to wear his cowboy clothes and his rough rider suit. Perhaps without the special train, the brass cannon and the khaki uniform he might not have become governor of New York in the hard fought campaign of 1898. The trip of the American fleet around the world; hunting for big game in Africa; seeking the River of Doubt in South America; raising a division of troops for the Great War; fighting libel suits with Barnes and an obscure Michigan editor,—he understood the strategic value of all such devices which a more timid person might have rejected.

TR AND THE PEOPLE

At one place in Dakota the train stopped to take water while we were at lunch.[3] A crowd soon gathered, and the President went out to greet them. We could hear his voice, and the cheers and laughter of the crowd. And then we heard him say, "Well, good-by, I must go now." Still he did not come. Then we heard more talking and laughing, and another "good-by," and yet he did not come. Then I went out to see what had happened. I found the President down on the ground shaking hands with the whole lot of them. Some one had reached up to shake his hand as he was about withdrawing, and this had been followed by such eagerness on the part of the rest of the people to do likewise, that the President had instantly got down to gratify them. Had the secret service men known it, they would have been in a pickle. We probably have never had a President who responded more freely and heartily to the popular liking for him than Roosevelt. The crowd always seem to be in love with him the moment they see him and hear his voice. And it is not by reason of any arts of

[3] John Burroughs, *Camping & Tramping with Roosevelt* (Boston: Houghton Mifflin Company, 1907), pp. 20–21. Burroughs is describing a trip he made with Roosevelt to Yellowstone Park in the spring of 1903.

eloquence, or charm of address, but by reason of his inborn heartiness and sincerity, and his genuine manliness. The people feel his quality at once.

*   *   *

We left [Washington] at 11 o'clock Thursday [February, 1909] and did not reach Hodgenville until about the same time Friday. . . .[4]
The President had a great reception at every town through which we passed. He rather expected a diminution of popular demonstration, I think, and for that reason gave the strictest orders that the time of our departure and the route would not be made public. For the first hour there were no yells, and it seemed to me the President saddened at the thought that it was the last trip he would take by rail as President and that he missed the demonstrations to which he had grown so accustomed. We did not have to wait long, however, before the whole country through which he was to pass knew the schedule time, and at each station there was always a great crowd to watch his train shoot by. At Altoona there must have been 5,000 people, and the same reception was given him at all the larger towns.

There were no stops to speak of, for we were travelling on a special train making record time. He jumped from his seat as readily for a half-dozen people at a road crossing as he would for a crowd at a station. As we would get a glimpse of some two or three people looking wistfully at his car we would call his attention to it, and he would pop up and be at the door in a minute waving his handkerchief, and the sight of that handkerchief was always a signal for a shout of welcome. . . .

I watched the upturned faces in every crowd he addressed or yelled "Good luck!" to, and there was always that unmistakable look of personal affection in the individual face as he appeared, and as he swept his eyes over the throng there was set up instantly, it seemed to me, a personal hand between him and every man or woman present. It was not the look which comes from admiration, and curiosity seemed to be absent entirely. It was purely one of affection. It made me think of a remark I heard Ambassador Bryce make only a few days ago:

"Nobody likes him now but the people."

PUBLIC IMPACT

The most remarkable social and political phenomenon observ-

[4] Lawrence F. Abbott, ed., *The Letters of Archie Butt, Personal Aide to President Roosevelt* (Garden City: Doubleday, Page & Company, 1924), pp. 335–37. Copyright 1924 by Doubleday, Page & Company. Reprinted by permission of Laura Abbott Dale.

able in this republic to-day is the immense and growing popularity of Theodore Roosevelt.[5] Through the large numbers of dispatches from the editors of Republican newspapers which we print this morning there runs this single note—the President's popularity is growing; he is to-day stronger with the people than ever before. The enthusiasm he has aroused asks no questions, demands no pledges, imposes no conditions. Its confidence, like its admiration, is boundless.

No American statesman ever had such an unquestioning support, a support so completely uncritical or one so manifestly due to the inspiration awakened by personality. It is an astonishing spectacle. To the renomination of President Grant in 1880 it was felt that the third-term tradition offered an insuperable obstacle. It will not in the slightest degree avail against the wave of popular favor that now promises to make Mr. Roosevelt the candidate next year. With the spirit he has invoked and stirred tradition counts for nothing. If the time for sobering up should be long deferred, we do not know that even institutions would count for very much.

* * *

Moreover, whatever his diversions in spelling, Mr. Roosevelt has left his impress on the language of the people in a few phrases which will outlast his physical life.[6] "The square deal," though drawn from the gaming-table, is quoted even in the pulpit. "Undesirable citizens" has a meaning more potent than any violent term of obloquy, and stands at the opposite extreme from "civic helpfulness." "The strenuous life," which he invented, and "the simple life," which he adapted, represent the two poles which keep our Americanism in equipoise. "The deliberate and malicious falsifiers" who have assailed him have been "beaten to a frazzle," and the "mollycoddles" have been set to study "latitude and longitude among reformers." The admonition, "Don't squeal, don't flinch; hit the line hard," calls up Mr. Roosevelt's passion for out-of-door sports. Here I must leave each reader to settle for himself the question whether the prize-ring, the football field, and the fastnesses of big game are the ideal places in which to teach sturdy manhood to the young; but the phrases drawn from them and engrafted into the speech of our every-day life by Mr. Roosevelt will undoubtedly survive with certain illustrative values even among the social element who take no delight in their sources. Their real suggestion, after all, is the importance of preserving one's bodily vigor, and letting no fear of results prevent any of us from taking his share in the rough-and-tumble of active life.

. . . Public opinion is what rules a republic like ours; at the founda-

[5] Editorial in the *New York Times*, August 7, 1907.

[6] Francis E. Leupp, "A Review of President Roosevelt's Administration. I—Its Human and Social Conditions," *The Outlook*, XCI (February 6, 1909), 307.

tion of all public opinion lies popular sentiment, and popular sentiment is made in the home rather than at the hustings. Hence my feeling that, whatever may have been his accomplishments in statecraft,
Theodore Roosevelt has performed a vastly larger, stronger, more important work even than guiding the destinies of our Nation; for he
has done more than any other President to shape the thought, the conduct, and the aspirations of the American people. He found them
veering away from the good old standards, and he has called them
back.

ROOSEVELT THE ADMINISTRATOR

Roosevelt's achievements as a public administrator have failed
of their due share of public appreciation.[7] His powers and his accomplishments in this respect were fully as remarkable as what he did in
the field of international statesmanship or as the leader of public
thought in America. His management and direction of the government machinery gave evidence of qualities as exceptional as those
which made him the unquestioned leader among advocates of personal
and civic righteousness.

As a public administrator Roosevelt gave proof of genius in the
selection of his assistants, in the formulation of great governmental
plans, and in securing a degree of efficiency in the conduct of the public business unmatched either before or since.

The corps of public officials whom Roosevelt drew around him during his presidency was probably without a parallel in the whole history
of government administration. They came from every walk of life, and
with every sort of background and training. But whether they were
public servants already in office when he became President, cowboys,
college graduates, frontiersmen, professors, gunmen, writers, scientists,
or professional executives, each one was distinguished by intelligent
loyalty to the government and to the ideals of the President, and by
that combination of devotion to duty and efficiency in service which
produces genuine results. . . .

Roosevelt used the whole Government of the United States consciously, and with the most conspicuous success, as a means of doing
good to the people of this country. The government to him was always a means to an end—never an end in itself—and he made use of
it, as he would of any other tool, for the accomplishment of very

---

[7] Gifford Pinchot, "Roosevelt as President," in Hermann Hagedorn, ed., *The
Works of Theodore Roosevelt*, National Edition, 20 vols. (New York: Charles Scribner's Sons, 1926), XV, xxviii–xxx. Copyright 1926 by Charles Scribner's Sons. Reprinted by permission of the publisher.

specific purposes, holding that whatever the people needed, and the law did not specifically forbid, he could do and ought to do.

In his own personal capacity to turn out work Roosevelt stood alone. . . .

What Roosevelt required of himself he required also, in their degree, of others. In consequence, the actual service rendered to the voters for each dollar of tax expended was immeasurably higher under Roosevelt than under any other of the seven national administrations with which I have been familiar. The driving power of the man at the head; the high and difficult standards which he set for himself; the generosity of his recognition of good work in others; his intimate acquaintance, not simply with the heads of departments, but with the work of subordinates throughout the Government Service; his unequalled power to arouse enthusiasm and command the very best each individual could produce—all these combined to transform, reanimate, and uplift the Government Service until it reached a point of efficiency where, in certain cases at least, government organizations had nothing to fear from comparison with the most effective organizations in the business world.

Roosevelt made it worth while to work for the people of the United States. He was the greatest of public administrators not only because his knowledge of the government was unrivalled, not only because he set in his own person a perfect example of effective work, not only because he was a great master of organization, but because he had the power to establish high ideals of public service, and to inspire in others the same devotion to the public good which illuminated his own life. Roosevelt never said: "Go you and serve the public while I watch you." He said: "Come on, let's do the job together."

THE NEW HAMILTONIAN

It is fortunate, consequently, that one reformer can be named whose work has tended to give reform the dignity of a constructive mission.[8] Mr. Theodore Roosevelt's behavior at least is not dictated by negative conception of reform. . . . No other American has had anything like so varied and so intimate an acquaintance with the practical work of reform as has Mr. Roosevelt; and when, after more than twenty years of such experience, he adds to the work of administrative reform the additional task of political and economic reconstruction, his originality cannot be considered the result of innocence. Mr. Roo-

[8] Herbert Croly, *The Promise of American Life* (New York: The Macmillan Company, 1909), pp. 167–71. Copyright 1909 by the Macmillan Company; renewed 1937 by the Macmillan Company. Reprinted by permission of the publisher.

sevelt's reconstructive policy does not go very far in purpose or achievement, but limited as it is, it does tend to give the agitation for reform the benefit of a much more positive significance and a much more dignified task.

Mr. Roosevelt has imparted a higher and more positive significance to reform, because throughout his career he has consistently stood for an idea, from which the idea of reform cannot be separated—namely, the national idea. He has, indeed, been even more of a nationalist than he has a reformer. . . . Fortunately, however, his aggressive nationalism did not, like that of so many other statesmen, faint from exhaustion as soon as there were no more foreign enemies to defy. He was the first political leader of the American people to identify the national principle with an ideal of reform. He was the first to realize that an American statesman could no longer really represent the national interest without becoming a reformer. . . . Mr. Roosevelt, however, divined that an American statesman who eschewed or evaded the work of reform came inevitably to represent either special and local interests or else a merely Bourbon political tradition, and in this way was disqualified for genuinely national service. He divined that the national principle involved a continual process of internal reformation; and that the reforming idea implied the necessity of more efficient national organization. Consequently, when he became President of the United States and the official representative of the national interest of the country, he attained finally his proper sphere of action. He immediately began the salutary and indispensable work of nationalizing the reform movement.

The nationalization of reform endowed the movement with new vitality and meaning. What Mr. Roosevelt really did was to revive the Hamiltonian ideal of constructive national legislation. . . .

Of course Theodore Roosevelt is Hamiltonian with a difference. Hamilton's fatal error consisted in his attempt to make the Federal organization not merely the effective engine of the national interest, but also a bulwark against the rising tide of democracy. The new Federalism or rather new Nationalism is not in any way inimical to democracy. On the contrary, not only does Mr. Roosevelt believe himself to be an unimpeachable democrat in theory, but he has given his fellow-countrymen a useful example of the way in which a college-bred and a well-to-do man can become by somewhat forcible means a good practical democrat. The whole tendency of his programme is to give a democratic meaning and purpose to the Hamiltonian tradition and method. He proposes to use the power and the resources of the Federal government for the purpose of making his countrymen a more complete democracy in organization and practice; but he does not make these proposals, as Mr. Bryan does, gingerly and with a bad conscience. He makes them with a frank and full confidence in an efficient national organization as the necessary agent of the national interest and purpose. He has completely abandoned that part of the traditional democratic creed which tends to regard the assumption by the government of responsibility, and its endowment with power adequate to the responsibility as inherently dangerous and undemocratic. He realizes that any efficiency of organization and delegation of power which is necessary to the promotion of the American national interest must be helpful to democracy. More than any other American political leader, except Lincoln, his devotion both to the national and to the democratic ideas is thorough-going and absolute.

As the founder of a new national democracy, then, his influence and his work have tended to emancipate American democracy from its Jeffersonian bondage. They have tended to give a new meaning to popular government by endowing it with larger powers, more positive responsibilities, and a better faith in human excellence. . . . Mr. Roosevelt has exhibited his genuinely national spirit in nothing so clearly as in his endeavor to give to men of special ability, training, and eminence a better opportunity to serve the public. He has not only appointed such men to office, but he has tried to supply them with an administrative machinery which would enable them to use their abilities to the best public advantage; and he has thereby shown a faith in human nature far more edifying and far more genuinely democratic than that of Jefferson or Jackson.

Mr. Roosevelt, however, has still another title to distinction among the brethren of reform. He has not only nationalized the movement, and pointed it in the direction of a better conception of democracy, but he has rallied to its banner the ostensible, if not the very enthusiastic, support of the Republican party. He has restored that party to some sense of its historic position and purpose. . . . The Republican party is still very far from being a wholly sincere agent of the national reform interest. Its official leadership is opposed to reform; and it cannot be made to take a single step in advance except under compulsion. But Mr. Roosevelt probably prevented it from drifting into the position of an anti-reform party—which if it had happened would have meant its ruin, and would have damaged the cause of national reform.

14

Roosevelt's Critics

A strong president inevitably makes enemies, and Roosevelt had his share. As a successful party leader he was naturally the beneficiary of much favorable comment among Republican politicians and in the columns of Republican newspapers. On the other hand, he was frequently attacked by Democratic politicians and editors. He provoked suspicion and hostility in other quarters as well. Some people resented TR's treatment of his opponents. Others were alienated by his egotism and self-righteousness. The following selections provide a sample of the partisan, sectional, and personal criticisms leveled at the twenty-sixth president.

SOUTHERN OPINIONS

In greater degree than that of any other President since the Negro was set free has Mr. Roosevelt's administration been the storm centre of the modern American race problem.[1] It is probably safe to say that he went into the White House without having given a thought to the question of formulating a "Negro policy." It is equally safe to say that he has not at any time in his official career been guilty of the childish whim of deliberately offending any section of the country. Yet before he had been in office many months he succeeded in offending the South as no other public man has done in recent years. Before a year had passed he had adopted a well-defined policy toward the political aspect of the race problem. This policy was simple enough. Its one tenet was that colour should not bar him from making political appointments. . . .

Three incidents marked the progress of the controversy which broke upon the country shortly after Roosevelt's succession to the presidency. These were the Booker Washington dinner, the appointment of Crum, and the closing of the Indianola post-office. . . .

The attitude of the South was one of general disapproval. In some instances the disapprobation was couched in violent and abusive terms.

[1] Alfred Holt Stone, *Studies in the American Race Problem* (New York, 1908), pp. 242–43, 245–46. Stone was a planter from the Yazoo delta of Mississippi.

In many the tone was one of dignified resentment. By some papers the [Booker T. Washington] affair was dismissed as not worth noticing. The one universal note was that the incident would have a harmful effect on the relations between the races.

* * *

The most damnable outrage which has ever been perpetrated by any citizen of the United States was committed yesterday by the President, when he invited a nigger to dine with him at the White House.[2] It would not be worth more than a passing notice if Theodore Roosevelt had sat down to dinner in his own home with a Pullman Palace car porter, but Roosevelt the individual, and Roosevelt the President, are not to be viewed in the same light. . . .

The President has rudely shattered any expectations that may have arisen from his announced intention to make the Republican party in the South respectable. He has closed the door to any accessions of Southern white men to the Republican ranks. They can no more ignore the instinct of race than can the bitterest Democratic bourbon.

* * *

In the face of the facts it can not but be apparent that the President's action was little less than a studied insult to the South, adopted at the outset of his Administration for the purpose of showing his contempt for the sentiments and prejudices of this section, and of forcing upon the country social customs which are utterly repugnant to the entire South.[3] In addition to all this, he is revivifying a most dangerous problem, one that has brought untold evil upon the whole country in the past, but which it was hoped, and believed, had been removed by the firmness and wisdom of the South.

OSWALD GARRISON VILLARD

I have already written elsewhere that Theodore Roosevelt did more to corrupt the press than anyone else.[4] By that I meant that he warped and twisted, consciously or unconsciously, by his fascinating personality the judgments of the best of the reporters and correspond-

[2] Memphis *Scimitar.* Quoted in *The Literary Digest,* XXIII (October 26, 1901), 486.

[3] New Orleans *States.* Quoted in *The Literary Digest,* XXIII (October 26, 1901), 487.

[4] Oswald Garrison Villard, *Fighting Years: Memoirs of a Liberal Editor* (New York: Harcourt, Brace and Company, 1939), pp. 151, 177–78, 181. Copyright 1939 by Harcourt, Brace and Company. Reprinted by permission of the publisher. Villard was the publisher of *The Nation* and the New York *Evening Post* and an independent reformer whom Roosevelt relegated to "the lunatic fringe."

ents and many of the editors. For example, Francis E. Leupp, for so many years *The Evening Post's* altogether admirable Washington correspondent, never lost the judicial attitude he sought to maintain until he succumbed to the charms of Theodore Roosevelt. He finally yielded to the President's blandishments, resigned, and accepted a federal office from him. . . .

Curiously enough, as the campaign [of 1904] waxed Theodore Roosevelt, the bold and the brave, became panic-stricken because of a fear that he was really in danger of defeat when there was no danger of that whatsoever. Defeat he could not face and so, yielding to his terror, he stooped to the most pitiful if not contemptible act of his career—he sold himself for campaign funds to the very Big Business men whom he had so long been calling, with truth, "the malefactors of great wealth." He sent for them, made terms with them, and the campaign coffers of the Republican Party were correspondingly enriched by a quarter of a million dollars. . . . He flatly denied, on November 4, the truth of the insinuation that Mr. Cortelyou had made use of knowledge gained in office to obtain contributions from corporations. He similarly denied that anyone "in my behalf and by my authority" had made any pledge or promise. He said that "it is a wicked falsehood" that "there has been any understanding as to future immunity or benefits in recognition of any contributions from any source." . . .

As soon as Mr. Frick heard the object of my coming he related the whole story with the utmost frankness. . . . He gave a graphic description of that early morning call at the White House and then said with astounding bluntness: "He got down on his knees to us. We bought the son of a bitch and then he did not stay bought."

JOSEPH L. BRISTOW

July 12 [1905].[5] My old friend, J. L. Bristow, formerly 4th Assistant Postmaster General and more recently Special Commissioner to Panama, visited me and spent several hours. He is on his way home to Kansas to take up his little country newspaper work again, after having done his country great service in great things.

He says Roosevelt has cast him ruthlessly aside after listening to the enemies against whom he had faithfully promised to protect him, when he appointed him to the work of running down some thieves. He said that he realized it would only injure him to express himself publicly as to the way he had been treated by Roosevelt and, therefore, would keep silent.

[5] Charles G. Dawes, *A Journal of the McKinley Years,* ed. Bascom N. Timmons (Chicago: R. R. Donnelley and Sons, 1950), pp. 405–6. Copyright 1950 by Charles G. Dawes and reprinted by permission of his heirs.

Bristow maintained that, in his friendships and personal relations, Roosevelt is insincere, subordinating all matters of personal loyalty or the rights of an individual (provided he be weak or too obscure to become a martyr in the public eye) to his own ambitions and interests. He says that his friendships are largely artificial, being based on self-interest chiefly—that he either over-praises or over-condemns—and that his desire for public applause over-rides his desire at times to give a weak man a square deal. In this I find Secretary Gage agrees with Bristow—in fact I suspect Roosevelt makes a hard man to work under.

RAY STANNARD BAKER

. . . [B]eginning in 1903, I was to have a voluminous correspondence and many lively meetings and conversations [with Theodore Roosevelt].[6]

President Roosevelt was greatly interested in my early labor articles. . . .

I was naturally greatly pleased that he should be impressed by my articles and that I had been able to contribute to his own knowledge of conditions, for he occupied the place of pre-eminent power in the United States, with a field of action and publicity far exceeding that of men like Carl Schurz. What he said echoed across the country, reaching people in every little hamlet and crossroad. What a thing it was, I thought, to have a President who was genuinely interested in these ugly aspects of our common life, and who was not afraid to attack them wherever they might be found. I became for a time his ardent and more or less uncritical follower.

But as the years passed Roosevelt's typical reaction, that of balancing the blame, without going to the root of the matter, and of seeking the "devil in the mess," satisfied me less and less. His actions often seemed to me to be based not upon principles well thought out, but upon moral judgments which were, or seemed to me to be, too hasty. His notion of a square deal was to cuff the radical on one ear and the conservative on the other, without enlightening either. He had no "single track mind"! He ran full-speed on all the tracks at once. Too often he rode down opposition without understanding what it meant, or talked it down with a torrent of phrases. But what energy and gusto he had, what wholesome enthusiasms, what common human goodnesses and courtesies!

[6] *American Chronicle: The Autobiography of Ray Stannard Baker* (New York: Charles Scribner's Sons, 1945), pp. 186–87. If there is a known address for Ray Stannard Baker, please notify Prentice-Hall, Inc., Englewood Cliffs, New Jersey. Baker was a leading journalist of the Roosevelt era and something of a muckraker. He later became the authorized biographer of Woodrow Wilson.

JOSEPH BENSON FORAKER

The tilt between the President and Senator Foraker at the Grid-iron dinner on Saturday night can not be ignored or silenced by club etiquette.[7] It was a battle royal.

The President saw fit to make an opening for attack and the Ohio Senator accepted the overture. The one preached a sermon on the duty of everyone to see the light as he saw it, and the other resented the encroachment, even of a President, upon the individual conscience.

Both the President and Senator were at their best. Mr. Roosevelt was forceful—more than strenuous—and cuttingly incisive. It is said to have been a speech of biting sarcasm, inter-larded with a vigorous vocabulary, ever at the President's wits' end. Those who sat under it knew instinctively that it would be countered.

It was taken by all who heard it as a direct challenge to Senator Foraker. More, indeed. It was taken as a lecture to him as an in-dividual and the Senate as a whole, reprobating both for stirring up the Brownsville mess. It was delivered in a high, strident pitch, and sandwiched with gestures more than emphatic.

During its delivery it provoked amazement at its audacity, won not a little applause, but to the knowing it carried apprehension and un-rest.

When Foraker arose to reply he was ashen white. He felt he had been singled out in a promiscuous company to be insulted. From the opening sentence he was more than virile. He did not mince words. He hurled back the gratuitous flings at himself and the Senate over his head. He denied even to a President the right to instruct him in his duties as a Senator. His review of the Brownsville episode was hardly felicitous, but it was keen and direct. His deduction that the final record of the case would be rightly adjudged was in a vein of wither-ing rebuke. . . .

[One witness reported]: "He first told Mr. Roosevelt that he would discover by the time the Senate concluded its investigation of the Brownsville case that the discussion in the Senate had been more than academic, and ventured to predict that the results would prove it.

"Then he read the President a lecture, which those who heard it will never forget. It was one of the most complete and effective ex-

[7] Washington *Post*, January 29, 1907. Reprinted by permission of the Washington *Post*. Joseph Benson Foraker, a Republican from Ohio and a United States senator from 1897 to 1909, opposed certain of the Roosevelt administration's policies and took the lead in a Senate investigation of the president's discharge "without honor" in November, 1906, of three Negro army companies accused of a shooting affray at Brownsville, Texas.

coriations I ever heard. Possibly the sting of the President's remarks was intensified by the knowledge that the friends of the administration in Ohio are trying to destroy him politically, although that is merely surmise on my part. Apparently he was inspired only by indignation. He declared with great dramatic effect that his oath of office was as sacred to him as was the President's to him, and no preachments from the White House were essential to the proper performance of his duty as a Senator."

BENJAMIN RYAN TILLMAN

Mr. President, the most marked feature of American politics at this time is the dominating influence and control of the executive branch of the Government over the legislative, and, in a less degree, over the judicial branches. . . .[8]

The Constitution lodges the power of appointment in the hands of the President, and the immense patronage of the office, amounting to millions and millions of dollars, has furnished an instrumentality with which to coerce Senators and Congressmen to acquiesce and yield obedience to the Executive will. The theory that the Senate must "advise and consent" before appointments are made is of little or no moment when Senators show such want of courage and self-respect and bow submissively to the orders from the White House. The members of the minority party are, of course, largely ignored. Appointments in the South, where the Democracy retains control, are in the hands of "referees," who fill the offices for the sole purpose of maintaining political machines. The Senators of the dominant party are afraid to resist the Executive will, lest they themselves should fail to obtain the patronage of their States. This condition is aggravated by the dread of Republican Senators lest the popularity of the President with the people shall force them into retirement if they resist the behests from the White House. When a clash between Senators or Members of the House has come, the people have sided with the President in almost every instance, and the fear of retirement from office through Presidential influence enables Mr. Roosevelt to pursue the policy of hectoring and domineering, which are the strongest features of his character. . . .

Turning from this aspect of the case, let us consider some of the facts known of all men which can not be ignored in making up a judgment as to the President's shortcomings and responsibilities. Mr. Roosevelt is always loud-mouthed and even vehement in the proclamation of his

---

[8] *Congressional Record*, 60th Cong., 1st sess. (March 16, 1908), pp. 3359–60. "Pitchfork Ben" Tillman, leader of the agrarian reformers in South Carolina in the 1880s and 1890s, served as governor of South Carolina, 1890–94, and as United States senator, 1895–1918.

own purity of purpose and patriotism. He has absolute faith in his own infallibility, and is apparently so drunk with power that he unconsciously lapses into the imperial "we" and sends cablegrams about "me and my people." But these things are of small moment—"vagaries of a noble and impetuous spirit"—and we could pass them by were it not for the existence of cold-blooded facts to show Executive responsibility for many of the evils which exist without dispute. The President clamors for changes in some old laws and enactment of new ones. The people, fretted and angry because of the wrongs to which they have been subjected, clamor with him. Some of these proposed changes are undoubtedly very desirable and necessary, but others appear to me to be most pernicious and dangerous. But of what use will it be to carry out these recommendations if the Executive himself fails to enforce the laws when enacted?

ROBERT MARION LA FOLLETTE

I state the facts here just as they transpired, because they illustrate the difference in methods which sometimes rendered it impossible for President Roosevelt and myself to cooperate on important legislation.[9] He acted upon the maxim that half a loaf is better than no bread. I believe that half a loaf is fatal whenever it is accepted at the sacrifice of the basic principle sought to be attained. . . .

Roosevelt is the keenest and ablest living interpreter of what I would call the superficial public sentiment of a given time and he is spontaneous in his response to it; but he does not distinguish between that which is a mere surface indication of a sentiment and the building up by a long process of education of a public opinion which is as deep-rooted as life. . . .

Roosevelt's attitude with reference to the coal land legislation in 1906, detailed in a previous chapter, is strikingly characteristic. He had encouraged me to believe that he would put back of this important legislation all the power of his administration. That encouragement led me in every speech I made during the recess, and I made many, to tell the story of the coal lands, the corrective legislation proposed, and of President Roosevelt's enthusiastic support. Upon my return to Washington at the beginning of the next session I found that, as promised, he had in his message recommended the legislation. After weeks of study and preparation, with the assistance of the Attorney General's department, a broad conservation measure was evolved which, when presented to Roosevelt, received his emphatic approval. But within

[9] *La Follette's Autobiography: A Personal Narrative of Political Experiences* (Madison, Wisc., 1913), pp. 387–89, 677–78. Copyright 1911, 1913 by Robert M. La Follette. Reprinted by permission of the Regents of the University of Wisconsin.

three days he had receded from his position. Because railroad and special interest Senators bitterly opposed the bill, as they were certain to do, and because they denounced me and my plan as socialistic, the President withdrew his support.

AMOS R. E. PINCHOT

Roosevelt was historically interesting as a politician of good character, fair intelligence, and high executive ability, whom a major economic interest, with a questionable system of acquisition to defend, felt obliged to corral by shrewd diplomatic approaches.[10] Because of his remarkable talents, his native sense of justice, his desire to play a righteous part in the eyes of the world, his unique genius in advertising his ideas, as well as himself, he should have been one of our greatest presidents. He failed first on account of the limitation of an unreflecting mind. He never got off by himself and thought things out to the end. The sessions of sweet silent thought were were not for him. He was too much on the go. He believed in action for action's sake— the strenuous life was his undoing. He failed in the second place because of the untoward accident that he came into power at the same moment when Morgan's mammoth steel consolidation came into being under the Damoclean sword of the Sherman law. Overcapitalized, oversized, a mushroom growth rather than a natural development, the Steel Corporation could live and prosper only through the maintenance of an illegal monopoly system built on differentials in transportation, fuel, and raw material. Bereft of these differentials, it would have been as helpless as a stranded whale. Morgan knew this; so did Gary and Perkins. That was the beginning of Roosevelt's undoing, if undoing there was. . . . But whatever may be the ultimate fate of his name, it will forever be associated in the minds of those interested in the inner workings of our politico-economic system with the simple formula set down at the beginning of this book: society in the industro-financial age is governed by wealth. Not wealth in every form, but surplus wealth over and above what is required to conduct business. . . . How innocent a pawn he was in the mighty and intricate system in which he was caught is a question on which we may differ, my own opinion being that he was surprisingly innocent about it. He had a talent for innocency. All things with which he associated himself fell in his mind easily into the category of goodness.

[10] Amos R. E. Pinchot, *History of the Progressive Party, 1912–1916,* ed. Helene Maxwell Hooker (New York: New York University Press, 1958), pp. 224–25. Copyright 1958 by the New York University Press. Reprinted by permission of the publisher. Pinchot was a brother of the more famous Gifford Pinchot and an ardent Progressive in 1912.

15
The Fun of Him

*One reason Theodore Roosevelt fascinated his contem-
poraries was the fact that he was an entertaining and amusing
public figure. The members of his generation could laugh with
him as well as at him, for he possessed a good sense of humor and
was capable of poking fun at himself. The strenuous Colonel
sometimes amused his fellow citizens when he did not intend to
do so; the intensity of his approach to life, the flamboyance of his
personality, and the relentless flow of his rhetoric were bound to
entrap such an activist again and again in situations that were
incongruous, controversial, or comic. Roosevelt developed the
capacity for what Elting E. Morison has called "the double-take,"
an ironic humor "that gives two images to reality—the event as
realized by the man acting in the event and as perceived by some
detached observer." By the mid-nineties, TR's friend Owen
Wister later recalled, "a wistfulness" had begun to lurk beneath
"the laughter and the courage of his blue eyes . . . ; but the
warmth, the eagerness, the boisterous recounting of some anec-
dote, the explosive expression of some opinion about a person,
or a thing, or a state of things—these were unchanged, and even
to the end still bubbled up unchanged."*

A RELUCTANT CANDIDATE

. . . Teddy has been here: have you heard of it?[1] It was more
fun than a goat. He came down with a sombre resolution thrown on
his strenuous brow to let McKinley and Hanna know once for all that
he would not be Vice-President, and found to his stupefaction that
nobody in Washington except Platt had ever dreamed of such a thing.
He did not even have a chance to launch his *nolo episcopari* at the
major. That statesman said he did not want him on the ticket—that
he would be far more valuable in New York—and Root said, with his
frank and murderous smile, "Of course not,—you're not fit for it."

[1] John Hay to Henry White, June 15, 1900, quoted in William Roscoe Thayer,
The Life and Letters of John Hay, 2 vols. (Boston: Houghton Mifflin Company,
1915), II, 342. Reprinted by permission of the Houghton Mifflin Company.

And so he went back quite eased in his mind, but considerably bruised in his *amour propre.*

MR. DOOLEY'S BOOK REVIEW

"Well sir," said Mr. Dooley, "I jus' got hold iv a book, Hinnissy, that suits me up to th' handle, a gran' book, th' grandest iver seen." [2] . . .

"What is it?" Mr. Hennessy asked languidly.

" 'Tis 'Th' Biography iv a Hero be Wan who Knows.' 'Tis 'Th' Darin' Exploits iv a Brave Man be an Actual Eye Witness.' 'Tis 'Th' Account iv th' Desthruction iv Spanish Power in th' Ant Hills,' as it fell fr'm th' lips iv Tiddy Rosenfelt an' was took down be his own hands. Ye see 'twas this way, Hinnissy, as I r-read th' book. . . .

. . . " 'I selected fr'm me acquaintances in th' West,' he says, 'men that had thravelled with me acrost th' desert an' th' storm-wreathed mountain,' he says, 'sharin' me burdens an' at times confrontin' perils almost as gr-reat as anny that beset me path,' he says. 'Together we had faced th' turrors iv th' large but vilent West,' he says, 'an' these brave men had seen me with me trusty rifle shootin' down th' buffalo, th' elk, th' moose, th' grizzly bear, th' mountain goat,' he says, 'th' silver man, an' other ferocious beasts iv thim parts,' he says. 'An' they niver flinched,' he says. 'In a few days I had thim perfectly tamed,' he says, 'an' ready to go annywhere I led,' he says. . . .

" 'We had no sooner landed in Cubia than it become nicessry f'r me to take command iv th' ar-rmy which I did at wanst. A number of days was spint be me in reconnoitring, attinded on'y be me brave an' fluent body guard, Richard Harding Davis. I discovered that th' inimy was heavily inthrenched on th' top iv San Joon hill immejiately in front iv me. . . . Wan day whin I was about to charge a block house sturdily definded be an ar-rmy corps undher Gin'ral Tamale, th' brave Castile that I afthwards killed with a small ink-eraser that I always carry, I r-ran into th' entire military force iv th' United States lying on its stomach. 'If ye won't fight,' says I, 'let me go through,' I says. 'Who ar-re ye?' says they. 'Colonel Rosenfelt,' says I. 'Oh, excuse me,' says the gin'ral in command (if me mimry serves me thrue it was Miles) r-risin' to his knees an' salutin'. . . . Ar-rmed on'y with a small thirty-two which I used in th' West to shoot th' fleet prairie dog, I climbed that precipitous ascent in th' face iv th' most gallin' fire I iver knew or heerd iv. But I had a few r-rounds iv gall mesilf an' what cared I? I dashed madly on cheerin' as I wint. Th' Spanish throops was dhrawn up in a long line in th'

---

[2] [Finley Peter Dunne], *Mr. Dooley's Philosophy* (New York, 1900), pp. 13–18.

formation known among military men as a long line. I fired at th'
man nearest to me an' I knew be th' expression iv his face that th'
trusty bullet wint home. It passed through his frame, he fell, an'
wan little home in far-off Catalonia was made happy be th' thought
that their riprisintative had been kilt be th' future governor iv New
York. Th' bullet sped on its mad flight an' passed through th' intire
line fin'lly imbeddin' itself in th' abdomen iv th' Ar-rchbishop iv
Santiago eight miles away. This ended th' war.'

" 'They has been some discussion as to who was th' first man to
r-reach th' summit iv San Juon hill. I will not attempt to dispute th'
merits iv th' manny gallant sojers, statesmen, corryspondints an'
kinetoscope men who claim th' distinction. . . . But I will say f'r
th' binifit iv Posterity that I was th' on'y man I see. An' I had a
tillyscope.' "

"I have thried, Hinnissy," Mr. Dooley continued, "to give you a
fair idee iv th' contints iv this remarkable book, but what I've tol' ye
is on'y what Hogan calls an outline iv th' principal pints. . . . I
haven't time f'r to tell ye th' wurruk Tiddy did in ar-rmin' an'
equippin' himself, how he fed himsilf, how he steadied himsilf in
battle an' encouraged himsilf with a few well-chosen wurruds whin
th' sky was darkest. Ye'll have to take a squint into th' book ye'ersilf
to l'arn thim things."

"I won't do it," said Mr. Hennessy. "I think Tiddy Rosenfelt is all
r-right an' if he wants to blow his hor-rn lave him do it."

"Thrue f'r ye," said Mr. Dooley, "an' if his valliant deeds didn't get
into this book 'twud be a long time befure they appeared in Shafter's
histhry iv th' war. No man that bears a gredge again' himself 'll iver
be governor iv a state. An' if Tiddy done it all he ought to say so
an' relieve th' suspinse. But if I was him I'd call th' book 'Alone in
Cubia.' "

SAGAMORE HILL

The Fourth of July was always the children's own day at Sagamore.[3] It began for the father of the family that first year of his
governorship at four in the morning, "by the thoughtfulness," as he
put it to a reporter later in the day, "of some youngster"—obviously
one of his own—"with a bunch of giant fire-crackers"; but he restrained his impulse to reach for the hair-brush when he remembered
similar "thoughtfulnesses" in his own boyhood. The Roosevelt chil-

[3] Hermann Hagedorn, *The Roosevelt Family of Sagamore Hill* (New York: The
Macmillan Company, 1954), pp. 83–84. Copyright 1954 by Hermann Hagedorn. Reprinted by permission of the publisher.

dren had strong views regarding a "safe and sane" observance of the nation's independence, which their father shared. But their elder playmate recognized the perils of gunpowder in inexperienced little fingers. Ignoring the Cuban fever which had racked him for three days running, keeping the punk-sticks lighted and forestalling casualties, he supervised all morning, from the piazza, what a *World* reporter called "the operations of a fire-cracker brigade, with Teddy, Jr., at the head of seventeen miniature rough riders from Cove Neck."

All evening he set off rockets, Roman candles and swishing, blazing pinwheels for an audience of thirty-three children gasping and squealing, dodging and shouting around him. "An enormous picture of Theodore in fireworks had been presented to us," Edith wrote Emily, "accompanied by the national salute of twenty-one bombs which quite overcame some of the smaller children." The long grass on the western slope was so dry that it caught fire a dozen times, and the father required all the exuberant energy of the children to help him put out the spreading flames.

Surely, when the last rocket had rushed up and burst in a shower of stars and the last Roman candle had feebly expelled its final fiery ball, he gathered the children in a great circle round him on the ground and told them of prairie fires that he and his cowboy companions had battled in the Bad Lands, splitting a steer and dragging the carcass at the end of a rope tied to a saddle, smothering a blaze here, only to see another rise roaring elsewhere, menacing cattle, horses, men, and the lonely ranchhouses where women stood watching, holding their children close. He knew how to tell such a story so boys would feel the sting of the smoke in their eyes and girls would see the flaming waves rushing nearer and nearer.

HIKING IN ROCK CREEK PARK

In Washington the President continued this practice of hiking, but in a somewhat modified form.[4] His favorite resort was Rock Creek, then a wild stream, with a good deal of water in it, and here and there steep, rocky banks. To be invited by the President to go on one of those hikes was regarded as a mark of special favor. He indulged in them to test a man's bodily vigor and endurance, and there were many amusing incidents and perhaps more amusing stories about them. M. Tardieu, who at that time was paying a short visit to this country and was connected with the French Ministry of Foreign

---

[4] Quoted in William Roscoe Thayer, *Theodore Roosevelt: An Intimate Biography* (Boston: Houghton Mifflin Company, 1919), pp. 261–63. Reprinted by permission of the Houghton Mifflin Company.

Affairs, told me that the dispatches which the new French Ambassador, M. Jusserand, sent to Paris were full of reports on President Roosevelt's personality. The Europeans had no definite conception of him at that time, and so the sympathetic and much-esteemed Ambassador, who still represents France at Washington, tried to give his Government information by which it could judge for itself what sort of a person the President was. What must have been the surprise in the French Foreign Office when it received the following dispatch: (I give the substance, of course, because I have not seen the original.)

> "Yesterday," wrote Ambassador Jusserand, "President Roosevelt invited me to take a promenade with him this afternoon at three. I arrived at the White House punctually, in afternoon dress and silk hat, as if we were to stroll in the Tuileries Garden or in the Champs Elysées. To my surprise, the President soon joined me in a tramping suit, with knickerbockers and thick boots, and soft felt hat, much worn. Two or three other gentlemen came, and we started off at what seemed to me a breakneck pace, which soon brought us out of the city. On reaching the country, the President went pell-mell over the fields, following neither road nor path, always on, on, straight ahead! I was much winded, but I would not give in, nor ask him to slow up, because I had the honor of *La belle France* in my heart. At last we came to the bank of a stream, rather wide and too deep to be forded. I sighed relief, because I thought that now we had reached our goal and would rest a moment and catch our breath, before turning homeward. But judge of my horror when I saw the President unbutton his clothes and heard him say, 'We had better strip, so as not to wet our things in the Creek.' Then I, too, for the honor of France, removed my apparel, everything except my lavender kid gloves. The President cast an inquiring look at these as if they, too, must come off, but I quickly forestalled any remark by saying, 'With your permission, Mr. President, I will keep these on, otherwise it would be embarrassing if we should meet ladies.' And so we jumped into the water and swam across."

EBULLIENT ROOSEVELT

I remember especially, as an example of the Colonel's methods in his later phase, a visit to his office in the early autumn of 1912.[5] After a rather long talk on the subject of the switch some of us had made to him, after La Follette's breakdown at the Publishers Dinner at Philadelphia, I descended in the elevator, only to discover that it was pouring with rain, and that I had left my umbrella in the Colonel's room. Taking an upgoing car, and landing, I think, on the

[5] Amos R. E. Pinchot, *History of the Progressive Party, 1912–1916* (New York: New York University Press, 1958), pp. 244–45. Copyright 1958 by the New York University Press. Reprinted by permission of the publisher.

seventh floor, I proceeded along the hall, when the Colonel, doubling the corner at breakneck speed, spied me and seized me by the hand. The conversation we had just had, momentous as it had seemed to me, had evidently entirely faded from his memory under stress of more important matters, as had also the trifling fact that he had said good-by to me but three minutes before. He greeted me as a new-comer, wrung my hand, beat me on the shoulder with his clenched fist, and asked with great effusiveness what he could do for me. "Why nothing, thanks," I replied, a little dismayed. "I was just going back to your office to get my umbrella. It's raining."

"Bully!" cried the Colonel, "Bully! Splendid! Bully! Come in and see me again any time." And at every word he showed his powerful teeth, snapped his muscular jaws, and continued to thump me, until, wheeling suddenly, he hurtled off with a triumphant upward wave of the hand.

16

The Progressive

Writing in March, 1912, a Bostonian who had recently served as Theodore Roosevelt's host during a meeting of the Harvard Overseers remarked that he had never seen the former president "in better physical shape. He is fairly stout, but his color is good, and he appeared vigorous. I saw no signs of unusual excitement. He halts in his sentences occasionally; but from a layman's point of view there was nothing to suggest mental impairment, unless the combination of egotism, faith in his own doctrines, fondness for power and present hostility to Taft . . . can be termed symptomatic." [1] *Roosevelt had entered the period of his most advanced progressivism, the future appeared to be filled with possibilities, and the dynamic Colonel was ardently eager to make the most of them. The selections below include a campaign vignette and a graphic recollection of the memorable Progressive convention that nominated Roosevelt for the presidency in August, 1912.*

CAMPAIGNING IN 1910

His first trip took him West to the Rocky Mountains and into the great Northwest.[2] This trip took him down South to Atlanta and out to St. Louis, through Tennessee, Georgia, Alabama, and Arkansas. . . .

And the South was nothing behind the West in the welcome it gave. The trip began on Thursday afternoon, and on Friday morning the first stop was made at Bristol, Tennessee. From an open stand in the center of a vacant lot, reached by strenuous efforts through a pushing, heaving mass of friendly people, Mr. Roosevelt made his first speech, or rather preached his first sermon. For in the South as in the North, in the East as in the West, he preached those simple doc-

---

[1] Robert Grant to James Ford Rhodes, March 22, 1912. In Elting E. Morison and associates, eds., *The Letters of Theodore Roosevelt,* 8 vols. (Cambridge, 1951–54), VIII, 1457.

[2] Harold J. Howland, "Down South and Back Again," *The Outlook,* XCVI (October 22, 1910), 384–86.

trines of good citizenship which those who fear him sneer at as platitudes, but which the people who listen to them receive with shouts of applause. . . .

. . . And at every stop Mr. Roosevelt, kind of heart and loth to disappoint any one, stepped to the rear platform, now for a mere wave of the hand or a scant word of greeting, now, when the stop was longer, for a brief exposition of the essentials of good citizenship. Time after time the scene was repeated, with small variations in the message, variations only of size in the audience, no variation whatever in the reception.

The train stops. The wave of men, women, and children flows about the rear platform; the thin, treble cheer goes up.

"I am glad to see so many of my fellow-citizens, especially those carrying little citizens in their arms." Laughter and cheers.

"You know my views on the baby question." Loud laughter and cheers.

"I like all your crops, but I like your baby crop best." Cheers.

"There are three essentials of good citizenship. The citizen must be honest; that is the foundation. He must have courage; I haven't much use for the good man who is timid. I hope we shall never come to a time when on one side of the community we have all the good men and on the other side all the courageous men. But those two qualities aren't enough. If a man's a natural-born fool, you can't do anything with him. To honesty and courage must be added the saving grace of common sense."

The train moves, hands clap, throats cheer, babies are lifted high to catch his eye, the characteristic smile from the rear platform has its response on every face. And so on to the next station.

At one stop a committee clambers over the rail and its chairman addresses the traveler, "We don't agree with you on all things, but we're just as glad to see you as if we did." A frank and graceful welcome, and quick as a shot comes back the rejoinder, "On the essentials of good citizenship we can all agree." There is no dissent, and the next statement, "A good American is a good American anywhere," brings out the cheers. . . .

If the evidence of threescore stops in four Southern States, and the welcome of threescore crowds, ranging in size from a corporal's guard to an army division, is of any value, the South likes Mr. Roosevelt just as does the West and the Northwest, and the East (outside of Wall Street and its sphere of influence). The South likes the man, it comes out to see him, it cries out, "There he is," when he appears, it cheers him, waves at him, smiles at him. And the South likes what he has to say, which is just the same that he has said in every State of the Union in which he has been in the past four months. This trip down South has been an impressive confirmation from the least likely quarter—the solid South—of the evidence given by the Western trip that Mr. Roosevelt's popularity knows no sectional lines.

THE BULL MOOSE

It may be excusable to pause in this narrative for a moment and write in some account of the Colonel as he appeared to me in that convention.[3] His wrath was submerged. He was ebullient, clicking his teeth sometimes like a snare-drum obbligato to the allegro of his blithe, humorous, self-deprecatory assurance. The squeaking falsetto in which he gently clowned himself was most disarming. He seemed full of animal spirits, exhaustless at all hours, exuding cheer and confidence. His paunch was widening a little. The cast of his countenance at rest was a little grimmer than it had been in those first days when I had known him as Assistant Secretary of the Navy and as a young President. Into him had come not merely the sense of power but the unconsciousness of power. For a decade I had noticed something magnetic about him. When he came into a room, he changed all relations in the room because perhaps all minds and hearts turned to him in some attitude, all differing perhaps, but influenced by him. There in Chicago, in the late summer of 1912, he was in command and yet was forever disclaiming, vaunting his modesty genially. With all his physical virility, he was indeed the Bull Moose charging about the hotel corridors, stalking down an aisle of the Coliseum while the crowds roared, walking like a gladiator to the lions. In those days of the accouchement of the Bull Moose, he was superb. What if he tried to cover and to defend Perkins? What if he was a little obvious now and then as he grabbed the steering wheel of events and guided that convention not too shyly? I felt the joy and delight of his presence and, knowing his weakness, still gave him my loyalty—the great rumbling, roaring, jocund tornado of a man, all masculine save sometimes a catlike glint, hardly a twinkle, in his merry eyes.

*   *   *

With these witnesses, fortified by my own experience, I have concluded that "Roosevelt progressivism" expressed more accurately the mass sentiment of my generation than the vague generalizations of the evangelic Bryan, the close reasoning of the uncompromising La-Follette, or the erudite radicalism of Wilson.[4] This "Roosevelt pro-

[3] *The Autobiography of William Allen White* (New York: The Macmillan Company, 1946), 489–90. Copyright 1946 by the Macmillan Company. Reprinted by permission of the publisher.

[4] Donald Richberg, *Tents of the Mighty* (New York and Chicago: Willett, Clark & Colby, 1930), 34–36. Copyright 1930 by Willett, Clark & Colby. Reprinted by per-

gressivism" did not question the existing order. It proposed changes in law, largely for the purpose of compelling or inducing men to be "good" instead of "bad." Public officials who behaved badly would be rejected, or their evil deeds would be annulled by popular vote. Employers would be directed to treat their employees well. Big business would be encouraged, if "good," and punished if "bad." The wicked strong people would be controlled and the good weak people would be protected.

This political program for bringing about "social justice" had several implications: (1) That there was a clear line between what was right and wrong. (2) That the People would vote right, if they had the chance. (3) That if public officials were responsive to public opinion, they would know what was right and would do it. . . .

But the "Roosevelt progressivism" was based on what the Colonel well called a "confession of faith." It had a creed. You accepted it and joined the church. And so the progressive national convention was a great revival meeting. Prosperity was the natural ideal—not for the few, as Roosevelt pointed out, but for the many. Government should lift the poverty-stricken to the happy level of the well-to-do. In this glorious hour of political intoxication, the prophet Beveridge cried: "Pass Prosperity Around"; and at once a banner, already painted with the new-born slogan, fell from the ceiling. If not a miracle, this was at least a miraculous conception. We wept and we cheered and we sang, "His truth is marching on."

---

mission of Harper & Row, Publishers, Inc. Richberg was a young Chicago lawyer and an ardent Progressive in 1912.

17
Partisan and Patriot

Theodore Roosevelt's final years were filled with discord and shrill complaint. Though still a magnetic figure, he no longer occupied the center of the stage, and his attitudes seemed less typical of the fundamental ideas of the great mass of Americans than was true in earlier years. His condemnation of Germany early in the war, his fervent support of preparedness, his declining interest in the Progressive party, his sharp criticism of President Wilson, and his intense nationalism frequently made his leadership divisive and caused many of his contemporaries to view him with suspicion if not hostility. Yet his hold on his fellow citizens was never entirely broken, and after the United States entered the war, his energetic labors for its prosecution cast him in a more constructive light. The following items touch on some of the developments involving TR during these final years.

ATTITUDE TOWARD GERMANY

. . . My break with Roosevelt was inevitable.[1] I saw him once more after this. In response to an impetuous letter, he invited me to see him. He told me that he wanted me to understand him, that I was the only one of his German American friends to whom he was willing to confide some of the underlying reasons for his anti-German attitude. He spoke fiercely, impressively. But his eloquence failed to convince me. "Germany," he reiterated, is a nation without a sense of international morality." I had England's innumerable violations of international law at my finger-tips. The Germans, he assured me, were plotting against us. He referred to Germany's alleged plans for invading this country. I replied that the German Army could not even swim across a narrow strip of the Channel! Deploring our "softness" and lack of preparedness, Mr. Roosevelt made the astonishing observation that it might be a good thing for Uncle Sam to receive a licking at the hands of the Germans. I could not agree with his

[1] George Sylvester Viereck, *Roosevelt: A Study in Ambivalence* (New York, 1920), pp. 113–14. Copyright 1919 by George Sylvester Viereck.

point of view. I did not believe in German intrigue. . . . I ceased to look upon Theodore Roosevelt as a friend.

AH! TEDDY DEAR

Ah, Teddy dear, and did ye hear the news that's goin' round? [2]

They say you're gone from off the stage, that strange cold men, whom we respect but love not, must be our meat for all the campaign days to come.

Gray is the prospect; dull is the outlook.

We felt all the while that over in the Auditorium and the Coliseum they were breaking to us the news of a death in the family. They were merciful; they held it back; they did not let us have the shock of it all at once. They meant kindly.

But now that the news has come the kindness of friends can help but little. Our hearts are broke! We need you and we want you every minute.

Ah the fun of you and the glory of you!

Where lies the American whose passion or whose imagination you have not set a-tingling? Who else has meant the savor of life for us? Who but you has taken us and set our feet upon the high places?

Before you came, all in politics was set and regular. Those who were ordained to rule over us did so with that gravity with which stupid grown-ups so oft repress the child. No one ever talked to us as you did. They called us "voters" or "constituents" or such big names as these. They never took us by the hand and laughed and played with us as you did. . . .

And then you came!

Dancing down the road you came with life and love and courage and fun stickin' out all over you. How we loved you at the first sight! And how you loved us! . . .

You told us of the birds in the air and of the fishes in the sea. The great tales of the old heroes, the sagas of the past, you spread before our 'stonished eyes. You gave us new words—delightful words—to play with; and jokes—delightful jokes—to make us laugh.

How we wanted you back when you went away! But they stole our right from us and they wouldn't let you come back. So we followed you. Four million of us, in a fight the like of which we never knew. Joy and religion were in it in equal measure. Hymns and cleanness

[2] Julian Mason, in the Chicago *Evening Post*, June, 1916. Quoted in Corinne Roosevelt Robinson, *My Brother Theodore Roosevelt* (New York: Charles Scribner's Sons, 1921), pp. 300–302. The Republican national convention had declined to nominate Roosevelt for president in 1916.

and color and battle all were jumbled in it. The good of it is set forever into the life of the nation.

But the schoolmaster beat you, and the Great War came to crowd you from our thoughts. We thought only of ourselves because you were no longer there to make us think of our country. At last we turned to you—when it was too late.

So now we are not to have you. We must go stumbling on alone, hoping that the man they've given us may show something of that fire and strength upon which you taught us to rely. . . .

But whatever you do or whatever you don't do, be sure of one thing—we shall never hold it against you. For all that is gone, you can do no wrong in our sight. The memory of you shall never fade from our hearts.

Ah, Teddy dear—we love you now and always.

CLEMENCEAU ON ROOSEVELT

If I have the temerity of addressing you it is because it may be permitted me to throw light on certain aspects which perhaps are not sufficiently clear to you.[3] Allow me to say, in all candor, that at the present moment there is in France one name which sums up the beauty of American intervention. It is the name Roosevelt, your predecessor, even your rival, but with whom there can now be no other rivalry than heartening success. I saw Roosevelt only once in my life. It was just after I left office and he returned from his lion hunt. He is an idealist, imbued with simple, vital idealism. Hence his influence on the crowd, his prestige—to use the right expression. It is possible that your own mind, inclosed in its austere legal frontiers, which has been the source of many noble actions, has failed to be impressed by the vital hold which personalities like Roosevelt have on popular imagination. But you are too much of a philosopher to ignore that the influence on the people of great leaders of men often exceeded their personal merits, thanks to the legendary halo surrounding them. The name of Roosevelt has this legendary force in our country at this time and in my opinion it would be a great error to ignore the force which everything counsels us to make use of as quickly as possible.

[3] Joseph Bucklin Bishop, *Theodore Roosevelt and His Time Shown in His Own Letters*, 2 vols. (New York, 1920), II, 427–28. Copyright 1920 by Charles Scribner's Sons; copyright renewed 1948 by Joseph Bucklin Bishop. Reprinted by permission of the publisher. In this open letter to Woodrow Wilson on May 27, 1917, France's Georges Clemenceau appealed to the president to reconsider his decision not to authorize Roosevelt to raise a division for service in France.

Roosevelt was one of the greatest craftsmen in the great laborious work which will constitute your glory. It cannot displease you that your two names are coupled in our minds. He, moreover, followed your idea. He wished to raise four volunteer divisions of infantry to be incorporated in our armies. The Senate and Congress did not withhold consent. If the law has charged you, Mr. President, with all the practical issues of the undertaking, it is no less true that Roosevelt represents a vast potential factor which a statesman is unable to overlook. Roosevelt cannot come alone, for his prestige on our battlefields demands that he come with prestige conferred on him by his countrymen. I claim for Roosevelt only what he claims for himself—the right to appear on the battlefield surrounded by his comrades.

We have just heard of the arrival of the first American unit on the front. All our hearts beat. With what joy our soldiers greeted the starry banner! Yet you must know, Mr. President, more than one of our poilus asked his comrade: "But where is Roosevelt? I don't see him." It is to convey this remark to you, not knowing whether my mission will reach you, that I have written this letter.

EDGAR LEE MASTERS VISITS SAGAMORE HILL

. . . Comes Roosevelt, and greets the man who leaves[4]
The taxi just ahead, then waits for me,
Puts a strong hand that softens into mine,
And says, O, this is bully!

                    We go in.
He leaves my antecessor in a room
Somewhere along the hall, and comes to me
Who wait him in the roomy library.
How are those lovely daughters? Oh, by George!
I thought I might forget their names, I know—
It's Madeline and Marcia. Yes, you know
Corinne adores the picture which you sent
Of Madeline—your boy, too? In the war!
That's bully—tea is coming—we must talk,
I have five hundred things to ask you—set
The tea things on this table, Anna—now,
Do you take sugar, lemon? O, you smoke!
I'll give you a cigar.

[4] From "At Sagamore Hill," in Edgar Lee Masters, *Starved Rock* (New York, 1919), pp. 95–97. Copyright 1919 by the Macmillan Company. Reprinted by permission of Mrs. E. L. Masters.

The talk begins.
He's dressed in canvas khaki, flannel shirt,
Laced boots for farming, chopping trees, perhaps;
A stocky frame, curtains of skin on cheeks
Drained slightly of their fat; gash in the neck
Where pus was emptied lately; one eye dim,
And growing dimmer; almost blind in that.
And when he walks he rolls a little like
A man whose youth is fading, like a cart
That rolls when springs are old. He is a moose,
Scarred, battered from the hunters, thickets, stones;
Some finest tips of antlers broken off,
And eyes where images of ancient things
Flit back and forth across them, keeping still
A certain slumberous indifference
Or wisdom, it may be.

But then the talk!
Bronze dolphins in a fountain cannot spout
More streams at once. Of course the war, the emperor,
America in the war, his sons in France,
The dangers, separation, let them go!
The fate has been appointed—to our task,
Live full our lives with duty, go to sleep!
For I say, he exclaims, the man who fears
To die should not be born, nor left to live.

A HERO GOES TO VALHALLA

We had been in the Hôtel Vouillemont only three days when
I came down to breakfast and saw in the morning edition of the Paris
Herald the news that Colonel Roosevelt was dead.[5] I can remember,
across the years, standing there with that paper in my hand; dumb,
speechless, and probably tearful. I could not have read that news
without sorrow. Again and again I looked at the headlines to be sure
that I was reading them correctly. Ray Baker came along, and I cried:
"Ray, Ray, the Colonel is dead—Roosevelt!"
He must have seen the grief in my face. He had the paper in his
hands also, for he had read it at breakfast. He put his hand on my
shoulder and said:
"Yes, Will, it's a great blow. We are all sorry."

[5] *The Autobiography of William Allen White* (New York: The Macmillan Company, 1946), p. 551. Copyright 1946 by the Macmillan Company. Reprinted by permission of the publisher.

Then he and Ida Tarbell and I sat down to talk it all over, and get used to a world without Roosevelt in it. Not since my father's death had grief stabbed me so poignantly as those headlines cut into my heart that gray, cold Paris morning.

PART THREE

ROOSEVELT IN HISTORY

>   *Theodore Roosevelt still commands the attention of
> the historian. Although his place in history has had its ups and
> downs during the half century since his death, it appears now
> to have become well established as a significant aspect of the
> nation's modern experience. Roosevelt was a vital force in the
> beginning of our own times. He was the first president to address
> himself seriously to the new industrial and urban problems. He
> both reflected and helped mold the thinking of the great middle
> register of Americans about the need for social analysis and
> action. Limited though his tangible accomplishments were, he
> nevertheless provided a remarkable demonstration of strong
> executive leadership in a democracy. The selections in this part
> of the book illustrate the wide range of historical opinion about
> the effervescent TR and touch upon the rehabilitation of his
> historical reputation during the years since World War II. They
> also reveal the appearance of a few sharply critical judgments on
> the twenty-sixth president during the recent period. Most of the
> items reprinted below are arranged in the order of their original
> publication.*

William Draper Lewis:
The Typical American

. . . We may admire a public man for the things he
has accomplished, for his brilliant and versatile ability; we may trust
him because we believe in the wisdom of his judgment; but our
affection only finds root in his character.[1]

Theodore Roosevelt was no exception to this rule. The attainments
of his mind, the exalted office which he held, the momentous char-

[1] William Draper Lewis, *The Life of Theodore Roosevelt* (Philadelphia and
Chicago, 1919), pp. 18–20, 22–23. All rights reserved. Reprinted by permission of
Holt, Rinehart and Winston, Inc.

acter of the work he accomplished all served but to bring him to the attention of mankind. Knowing him, people loved him, not for these things, but for certain great qualities of character expressed in his high sense of honor, his burning hatred of injustice, his deep sense of the obligation for personal service and, above all, his intense love for his country.

Again, perhaps, not a little of our affection for him arose from the fact that he was very human, which is only another way of saying that he had faults. . . .

Roosevelt is our typical American. Not that we are like him, but in that the worker in field, forest, mill and office, irrespective of financial position and social standing, sees in this great scholar and statesman, this vigorous, hearty, courageous out-of-door man, with his high ideals and intense love for the everyday simple things of life, the embodiment of a type which, above all others, he admires. . . .

Neither do we need the perspective of time to learn the simple, but all-important, lessons of the main events of his life. These events speak for themselves. They need no comment or criticism to teach again the need for hard work and often of great courage to attain any end which is worth while; or to impress on us the age-old truth that opportunity, though she may come in an unexpected form, comes only to him who is prepared to meet her. Men marvel at the great amount of work he accomplished. There are two reasons: One is found in the fact that his youthful struggle against delicate health had given him a sound body to be the servant of his restless energy; the other is that he cultivated his tastes and ordered his time so that, though he played more than most busy men and usually obtained sufficient rest and relaxation, he never wasted or frittered away his time. The value of the conservation of time, of the relaxation which comes from complete change of mental occupation especially after moments of intense excitement, is the lesson he taught everyone who came into working contact with him. . . .

As he saw the truth, so he spoke it. It was not that he did not care for his own future, or was not accustomed to consider the effect of word or action. On the contrary, as a politician, he wanted support from all kinds of people, and he was always willing to use every honorable means to secure support for himself, his party or his political ideals. He was a past master in the art of handling men, and making them do what he wanted them to do. But by conscious effort, as a young man, he had so schooled himself that he never balanced what he regarded as right to say or do against its possible effect on his own fortune. No man was so highly placed in the political or business world that he feared to publicly condemn him. No interest or class was so powerful that it could control his action against his judgment. . . .

Like all other of our great statesmen who have won a permanent place in the affections of the people, he had an intense love for his country. It is said that his whole life was an expression of "Jubilant Americanism." And this is so, if by it we mean that his life was an exuberant expression of dynamic force, a triumphant assertion of his country's greatness. With him, this love for country was based on complete knowledge. He knew his country's history as few men knew it. No other public man of his own or any other time was so intimately and personally acquainted with the conditions environing the life, with the outlook, and with the best aspirations of so many different classes. He could count among his personal friends officers of the army and navy, diplomats, publicists, professors, naturalists, hunters of big game, editors, explorers, ranchmen, social workers, captains of industry, labor leaders, Catholic priests, Protestant clergymen and Jewish rabbis. He was personally acquainted with every part of the country. His campaign trips had taken him to every state and to every town of consequence. He had spent summers in the Maine woods and on the Western plains; he had hunted grizzlies in the Rockies, visited remote Indian tribes in the great American desert, drilled troops in Texas, and herded cattle on the Little Missouri. At will he could visualize and describe the physical aspect of any mountain, stream, plain or desert he had ever seen, as only those can who are at once, as he was, a good naturalist, a keen huntsman and a lover of nature.

John Chamberlain:
The Moralist as Politician

Roosevelt's inheritance bred in him a certain philosophical irresponsibility.[2] He was not interested in ideas—which is to say that he was a careerist, a showman of his own personality. He might have gone the way of so many of his fellows; he might have dabbled in the law, done a little hunting, followed the migrations of the social seasons. His showmanship might have been limited to chasing the fox with superior skill; it might have been circumscribed by yachting at Newport or on Long Island Sound. But a weak body, shaken in youth by recurrent spasms of asthma, and weak eyes that rendered him unfit for baseball or football, caused him to rebel against his physical heritage in such a way that he exalted a certain synthetic primitivism; he must climb mountains, jostle with cowboys on the round-up, meet the "bad men" on their own ground and on their own terms. . . .

By stepping out of his social context, Roosevelt was forced to make a game of life. His background of inherited wealth, with its assumed concomitant of *noblesse oblige,* engendered in him, it is true, a certain feeling of responsibility; but it was never whole-souled. Since he was making a gift of his life to the commonweal, since he was playing a game, there were privileges he might assume, laurels he might demand for the victory. He was making a career; the career should make him.

And so, at crucial moments, consistency, proclaimed philosophical principle, the assumptions he made at beginning points and in his books on ideals, went casually by the board. "Get action," he said, "do things; be sane, don't fritter away your time; create, act, take a place wherever you are and be somebody; get action." But (so a philosophically responsible person might ask) action for what? . . . Do what things? . . . Be sane in what way, and for what reason? . . .

Certainly Roosevelt had no realistic definition of government, no philosophical grasp of the nature of politics. Politics, by definition, is primarily the organization by legislation and control of the means of life; it is based pretty largely on economic desires and it reacts upon economics in turn. An "economic agnostic" has no more business running for legislative or executive office than an ibis has at the North

[2] John Chamberlain, *Farewell to Reform: The Rise, Life and Decay of the Progressive Mind in America,* 2nd ed. (New York, 1933), pp. 235–38, 266–68, 271–72. Copyright 1932 by John Chamberlain. Reprinted by permission of the John Day Company, Inc.

Pole. But Roosevelt, the "agnostic" ("I do not know"), never had any hesitation about injecting himself into the forefront of the political fight. Like so many Americans who were still confusing the imperatives of the stomach with the voice of God, he conceived of politics as a sphere for the dramatics of Protestant morality. The result was a vast confusion about standing at Armageddon (with Boss Bill Flinn of Pittsburgh) and battling for the Lord (who was on the side of the biggest slush fund). And the worst of it is, Roosevelt was perfectly sincere about his Armageddon stuff at the moment of utterance. . . .

Roosevelt was always willing, at any time, to contradict himself, by word or deed, if by contradiction he could further his career. His friends will be quick to say, "No, no." But there are so many major issues on which he shifted ground at the precise moment when his career was involved that charity balks at the attempt to find excuses. He became a Progressive when the Republican Party threatened to become Progressive—but it should not be forgotten that he fought La Follette in Wisconsin in 1904, and he was willing to enter a "gentleman's agreement" with Nelson Aldrich not to disturb the McKinley home policies if he could have a free hand in the conduct of foreign affairs. He reversed himself on free trade early in his career. This would be understandable as a natural growth—only Roosevelt never had any real conviction on the tariff, one way or another. His attitude, when President, was "Let Taft change the tariff when I'm gone"; but when Taft compromised with Aldrich and the Bourbons of the Senate, Roosevelt lapsed into an unholy rage. He denounced the "corrupt" Blaine; but when Blaine was nominated, in 1884, the willing worker in the vineyard decided that Cleveland, the friend of Civil Service reform, was the real instrument of Satan. And when Blaine became Harrison's Secretary of State, Roosevelt was quite willing to play up to him for a job. . . .

Roosevelt could always take a high moral tone; he repeatedly showed himself on the side of righteousness, even though humanity might, at times, go hang. But even in the matter of morality, expediency altered cases. The young Governor of New York State temporized on the Erie Canal frauds. As President, Roosevelt was perfectly willing to use party machinery to dictate Taft's nomination, yet in 1912 he called Elihu Root a thief for exercising the same prerogative in throwing out the Roosevelt delegates. When John Hay negotiated the Hay-Pauncefote treaty, Roosevelt didn't like it, and argued that a government had the right to abrogate a treaty in a "solemn and official manner." But when Colombia refused to accept the Hay-Herran treaty, Roosevelt quickly doubled on his tracks and denounced the Bogatá "dagoes," as he called them, for "breach of faith." . . .

All the chopping and changing, the roaring invocations to morality and the sudden descents to political bargaining, simply prove to me that Roosevelt was a surface swimmer—not so brave a man as Grover Cleveland, and neither so honest as Boies Penrose on the one hand, nor as La Follette, on the other. He was, it is clear, the perfect *representative* of the middle class of pre-War America. His class philosophy, however, was inchoate—in no way so clearly formulated as La Follette's. . . .

Roosevelt's domestic achievements were more ethical than the Panama intrigue. But his two administrations were more talk than effort; Taft's "progressive record" is fully as clean as Roosevelt's own. . . .

A final estimate of Roosevelt, I think, will be that expressed by Senator Aldrich: he was the greatest politician of his time. Not, mind you, the greatest statesman—not even by the test of action, which John Carter makes the one test of statesmanship. And no one has succeeded in endowing Roosevelt with economic sense; the judgment of Gardner, that he kept himself an economic moron in order to remain in politics, must stand. So let him rest—as a great politician and an astounding, charming, effervescent character. But what an ironic role to be played by a moralist!

Richard Hofstadter:
Stabilizer of the Status Quo

The ambiguity that can be seen in his trust policies came naturally and honestly to Theodore Roosevelt.[3] In his early days it had always been his instinct to fight, to shoot things out with someone or something—imaginary lovers of his fiancée, Western Indians, Mexicans, the British navy, Spanish soldiers, American workers, Populists. But before he became President he had learned that an ambitious politician must be self-controlled and calculating. His penchant for violence, therefore, had to be discharged on a purely verbal level, appeased by exploding in every direction at once. The straddle was built like functional furniture into his thinking. He was honestly against the abuses of big business, but he was also sincerely against indiscriminate trust-busting; he was in favor of reform, but disliked the militant reformers. He wanted clean government and honest business, but he shamed as "muckrakers" those who exposed corrupt government and dishonest business. (Of course, he was all in favor of the muckrakers' revelations—but only if they were "absolutely true.") "We are neither for the rich man nor the poor man as such," he resounded in one of his typical sentences, "but for the upright man, rich or poor." Such equivocations are the life of practical politics, but while they often sound weak and halting in the mouths of the ordinary politician, Roosevelt had a way of giving them a fine aggressive surge.

Roosevelt had a certain breadth and cultivation that are rare among politicians. He read widely and enthusiastically, if not intensely, remembered much, wrote sharply at times and with a vivid flair for the concrete. He had generous enthusiasms. He invited Booker T. Washington to the White House, elevated Holmes to the Supreme Court, and gave Edwin Arlington Robinson a political sinecure. Thoughtful and cultivated men found him charming, and it is hard to believe that this was merely because, as John Morley said, he was second in interest only to Niagara Falls among American natural phenomena. Yet those who knew him, from shrewd political associates like Root to men like Henry Adams, and John Hay and Cecil Spring Rice, refused to take him altogether seriously as a person. And rightly so,

[3] Richard Hofstadter, *The American Political Tradition and the Men Who Made It* (New York: Alfred A. Knopf, Inc; London: Jonathan Cape, Ltd., 1949), pp. 225–28. Copyright 1948 by Alfred A. Knopf, Inc. Reprinted by permission of the publishers.

for anyone who today has the patience to plow through his collected writings will find there, despite an occasional insight and some ingratiating flashes of self-revelation, a tissue of philistine conventionalities, the intellectual fiber of a muscular and combative Polonius. There was something about him that was repelled by thoughtful skepticism, detachment, by any uncommon delicacy; probably it was this that caused him to brand Henry James and Henry Adams as "charming men but exceedingly undesirable companions for any man not of strong nature," and to balk at "the tone of satirical cynicism which they admired." His literary opinions, which he fancied to have weight and importance and which actually had some influence, were not only intolerably biased by his political sentiments but, for all his proclaimed robustiousness, extremely traditional and genteel. . . .

The role in which Roosevelt fancied himself was that of the moralist, and the real need in American public life, he told Lincoln Steffens, was "the *fundamental fight for morality*." . . . This was accurate enough; Roosevelt's chief contribution to the Progressive movement had been his homilies, but nothing was farther from his mind than to translate his moral judgments into social realities; and for the best of reasons: the fundamentally conservative nationalist goals of his politics were at cross-purposes with the things he found it expedient to say, and as long as his activity was limited to the verbal sphere the inconsistency was less apparent.

His mind, in a word, did not usually cut very deep. But he represented something that a great many Americans wanted. "Theodore Roosevelt," said La Follette caustically, "is the ablest living interpreter of what I would call the superficial public sentiment of a given time, and he is spontaneous in his reactions to it." What made him great, commented Medill McCormick, was that he understood the "psychology of the mutt." While Bryan had been able to do this only on a sectional basis, Roosevelt spoke the views of the middle classes of all parts of the country, and commanded the enthusiastic affection of people who had never walked behind a plow or raised a callus. He had a special sense for the realities they wished to avoid; with his uncanny instinct for impalpable falsehoods he articulated their fears in a string of plausible superficialities. The period of his ascendancy was a prosperous one, in which popular discontent lacked the sharp edge that it had had when Bryan rose to prominence. Although the middle classes, which contributed so much to the strength of progressivism, were troubled about the concentration of power in political and economic life and the persistence of corruption in government, it is doubtful that many middle-class men would have been more willing than Roosevelt to face the full implications of an attempt to unravel the structure of business power, with the attendant risk of upsetting a going concern. The general feeling was, as Roosevelt wrote Sir George

Trevelyan in 1905, that "somehow or other we shall have to work out methods of controlling the big corporations *without* paralyzing the energies of the business community."

This sentence is characteristic of the essentially negative impulses behind Roosevelt's political beliefs. It was always: We shall have to do this in order to prevent that. Did he favor control of railroad rates more because he was moved to correct inequities in the existing tolls or because he was afraid of public ownership? Did he force the mine operators to make a small concession to their employees because he bled for the men who worked the mines or because he feared "socialistic action"? Did he advocate workmen's compensation laws because he had a vivid sense of the plight of the crippled wage earner or because he was afraid that Bryan would get some votes? "There were all kinds of things of which I was afraid at first," he had said of his boyhood, ". . . but by acting as if I was not afraid I gradually ceased to be afraid." But did he lose his fears, or merely succeed in suppressing them? Did he become a man who was not afraid, or merely a man who could act as though he was not afraid? His biographer Henry Pringle has pointed out how often he actually underwent attacks of anxiety. In his anxieties, in fact, and in the very negative and defensive quality of his progressivism, may be found one of the sources of his political strength. The frantic growth and rapid industrial expansion that filled America in his lifetime had heightened social tensions and left a legacy of bewilderment, anger, and fright, which had been suddenly precipitated by the depression of the nineties. His psychological function was to relieve these anxieties with a burst of hectic action and to discharge these fears by scolding authoritatively the demons that aroused them. Hardened and trained by a long fight with his own insecurity, he was the master therapist of the middle classes.

Russel B. Nye:
Publicist of Reform

Roosevelt's real contribution to Midwestern progressivism did not come from the fact that he was part of it, for he was not, nor from what he accomplished for it, for he accomplished little.[4] It lay instead in the leadership he assumed in the progressive movement at large, a leadership that the Midwest accepted with reservations, but nevertheless accepted. There was in the nation in 1900 a vague but powerful drift toward honest, efficient, and representative government. Roosevelt became its spearhead. Whether he led the way or whether he stepped in at the head of a procession that had already formed (Roosevelt believed the latter) is beside the question. He was important to progressivism because he was to his eternal credit the first President after the Civil War who had more than an inkling of what had happened to the nation socially, politically, and economically since 1865. He dramatized the conflict between progressivism and conservatism, made it alive and important, and caught the imagination of the people with it, even though he did not resolve it. For reasons of temperament he was unable to resolve it, since much of his progressivism was verbal and he could never bring himself to translate it into concrete terms. His principles dissolved too often into glittering generalities. "We are neither for the rich man nor the poor man as such, but for the upright man, rich or poor," is a cheeringly progressive and impeccably liberal statement, but one difficult to put into law books. Yet his contributions to the rising wave of progressivism were not inconsiderable. The teeth, the eyeglasses, the bouncing vitality, the "big stick" and the "strenuous life," the St. George-like sallies against the trusts—all of these were trademarks of a muscular, youthful, aggressive, optimistic democracy that captured the nation's fancy. The real progressivism of Roosevelt never came close to the ideal, but at least the ideal was there for others to pursue.

Roosevelt's failure as a real progressive leader in the period 1900 to 1908 was the result of certain traits in his own character that were liabilities as well as assets. He was all things to everybody, something a reformer cannot be. To the rich he was a wealthy young country squire who held some unsound ideas but who would no doubt grow out of them. To the antirich he was the energetic pursuer of the

[4] Russel B. Nye, *Midwestern Progressive Politics: A Historical Study of Its Origins and Development, 1870–1950* (East Lansing, Mich., 1951), pp. 250–51. Copyright 1951 by the Michigan State College Press. Reprinted by permission of the publisher.

"malefactor of great wealth." To the trust he was a man with the laudable purpose of smashing the "bad" trust, but none considered themselves bad. Roosevelt was therefore often led to compromise in order to maintain his standing as an all-round political athlete. "The men who wish to work for decent politics," he wrote in 1904, "must work practically . . . ," a principle he held through his entire career. There was in him none of the tenacity, the grimness, the relentless rectitude that was La Follette's strength as a leader and one of his political weaknesses. "How I wish I wasn't a reformer, oh, Senator!" he wrote Chauncey Depew. "But I suppose I must live up to my part. . . ." Roosevelt compromised in order to live; La Follette could not compromise and live.

Roosevelt also had more than his share of what Mark Twain called "the circus side of a man's nature." He was an inveterate showman, unable to resist a scene even if it meant a slight stretching of principles. His pursuit of his quarry resembled a Long Island fox hunt, in which the fox was brought to earth amid great hallooing but released to run again another day. He was a spectacular man, taking San Juan Hill, stalking lions or trusts, scolding the "mollycoddles," but never quite making anything more than a game of it. It is hard to imagine Roosevelt sitting down, as La Follette did a few years later, with a mountain of records night after night to become a tariff expert in a few weeks in order to defeat a bad tariff bill. Nor is it any easier to imagine Roosevelt continuing any political battle, as La Follette did, for twenty-four years, or leading a new party at seventy. But Roosevelt in 1904 probably represented better than La Follette what the public wanted. The mass of the people did not quite know which way to turn in the titanic conflict between progressivism and the interests, and Roosevelt quite honestly reflected that indecision. People in general feared the trust and the specially privileged, but not quite enough to demand decisive action, and Roosevelt acted precisely as the public felt. As one of his advisers put it bluntly and truthfully, his real power came from the fact that he "understood the psychology of the mutt."

Eric F. Goldman:
Patrician Reformer

As President, Roosevelt was certainly no paragon of reform.[5] He could be brutally militaristic, evasive about trusts, compromising on social legislation, purblind to the merits of reformers who did not equate reform with Theodore Roosevelt. Yet the bouncing Teddy, with his bold grasp of the possibilities in change, his instinct for workable political combinations, his teeth-gnashing phrases, was the most tremendous thing that could have happened to American progressivism. Before a dazzled country, Roosevelt preached the progressive doctrine of executive leadership. The leadership, however much it wobbled, moved in the general direction of the use of federal powers to promote clean, efficient government, to check exploitation by large-scale capital, and to strengthen the bargaining position of lower-income groups.

Lashing out at "malefactors of great wealth," Roosevelt revived the Sherman Antitrust Law and employed it in a way that made trust magnates more careful even if the general concentration of industry was not appreciably slowed. By persistent conservation propaganda, he secured from Congress sweeping powers to remove public lands from the possibility of plundering operations, and used the powers to withdraw 148,000,000 acres of forest lands, 80,000.000 acres of coal lands, 4,700,000 acres of phosphate lands, and 1,500,000 acres of potential waterpower sites. With Presidential co-operation, often with Presidential goading, Congress forbade railroad rebates, strengthened the Interstate Commerce Commission, passed a meat-inspection act and a pure food and drug law, and brought the federal government into the workmen's compensation field for the first time. When intransigent owners produced a national coal strike, the country witnessed an unprecedented scene. Cracking down on the operators and forcing them to arbitrate, Roosevelt pulled the federal government far from its accustomed business-is-always-right position.

A whole new attitude permeated the White House. Since the days of Grant, the typical visitor had been a politician with a state in his pocket or a banker come to deal on equal, if not superior terms with the President. Roosevelt was openly sniffish about big businessmen;

[5] Eric F. Goldman, *Rendezvous with Destiny: A History of Modern American Reform* (New York, 1952), pp. 163–65. Copyright 1952 by Alfred A. Knopf, Inc. Reprinted by permission of the publisher. The footnotes in the original passage have been omitted.

they needed "education and sound chastisement." While never neglecting the politicians, he always managed to convey the impression that he found them a decidedly inferior lot. He didn't want the Vice-Presidency, Roosevelt kept telling the delegates who were making him Vice President with no real effort on his part to stop them. "I couldn't stand those damned Senators. I'd be throwing the gavel at them." During the Roosevelt Administrations the White House calendar was crowded with the names of artists, writers, professors, anyone with an idea, particularly a new and startling idea. The President wrote introductions to dissident books like Ross's *Sin and Society,* named that persistent nonconformist, Oliver Wendell Holmes, to the Supreme Court, and, for the first time in the history of American cabinets, appointed a Jew to his official family.

These Roosevelt attitudes ran all up and down the spine of the federal government, attracting to its service men of the honesty, abilities, and broad social view, for which reformers had pleaded so long. Until 1906 the federal District Attorney's office in southern New York, the most important in the United States, had usually been manned by lawyers of so little talent that the government hired outside attorneys when an important case was involved. He wanted, Roosevelt shrilled, the legal help of some of "my type of men," and the call was answered by Henry L. Stimson and a group of able young assistants, including Felix Frankfurter. On a total budget that was less than Stimson alone had earned in private practice, the new group converted the Southern New York office into the equal, if not the superior, of any corporation legal staff in the country.

For thousands who did not enter the government, Roosevelt was a bombshell. America of the early 1900's did not easily dismiss an agitator who bore one of the nation's most aristocratic names, who could charm a Sunday-school class or lead a regiment, turn out historical essays or lasso a steer, and who, in addition, happened to be President of the United States. In Emporia, Kansas, subscribers to the *Gazette* were reading strange doctrine. What was the matter with Kansas, William Allen White was saying now, was not reformers but "special privilege," and White was going down the line for the whole progressive program. "I was a young arrogant protagonist of the divine rule of the plutocracy," White recalled in 1934. Roosevelt "shattered the foundations of my political ideals. As they crumbled then and there, politically, I put his heel on my neck and I became his man."

"Teddy," White added, "was reform in a derby, the gayest, cockiest, most fashionable derby you ever saw."

Elting E. Morison:
Roosevelt as a Conservative

. . . From the crowded ledger of the Roosevelt years, three things may be extracted for further consideration.[6] First, some surprisingly accurate intuitive judgments on matters both great and small. The hips that Lincoln Steffens said that Roosevelt thought with turned out to be quite sensitive instruments. As John Hay said, "he raises intelligence to the quick flash of intuition." Feeling, as he did, that the problems of the time were produced by the push of unorganized industrial energy, Roosevelt set about first to assist where he could in the passage of specific laws to conserve and develop our resources, to regulate common carriers, to dissolve monolithic corporate structures, in short to bring the industrial energy within an organized control. Anyone who takes the trouble to read the letters in these volumes will discover how carefully Roosevelt proceeded in his effort to obtain laws designed at once to satisfy the prejudices of Congress, to protect the rights of the public, and to fulfill the legitimate requirements of industry. And in these letters may also be discovered how he sought to strengthen old and to create, where necessary, new agencies through which the laws might be administered with speed and decision.

At the same time in external affairs, he discerned that the future of the country lay within the whole world and not in some insulated corner. He therefore, without nostalgic allegiance to a provincial past or self-deceiving and sentimental pretensions that this was the white man's burden, set about—in so far as he could—to equip the country for international maturity. The great island administrations of his Presidency were honest, sound, and without imperial illusion in seeking to encourage wherever possible the active participation of the island populations in government. In the Orient, in South America, in Europe he acted with decision and with flair to maintain the position or to express the interest of his country in world affairs. In further support of position and interest he sought by reason, political maneuver, and indeed by guile to build a naval force sufficient to continue our policies by other means, should conference and negotiation fail.

[6] Elting E. Morison, "Introduction," in Morison and associates, eds., *The Letters of Theodore Roosevelt*, 8 vols. (Cambridge: Harvard University Press, 1951–54), V, xviii–xxii. Copyright 1951, 1952, 1954 by the President and Fellows of Harvard College. Reprinted by permission of the publisher.

To some observers this shrill concern with the length of the battle line suggested that Roosevelt sought to obtain his ends exclusively by reeking tube and iron shard. There is no doubt that he respected, perhaps unduly, military power, but he argued, in season and out, that our real strength in foreign affairs derived from a combination of physical, intellectual, and moral energy—that is from our total national character.

No doubt in the field of international relations as elsewhere, the claims were greater than the substance; no doubt, as at Portsmouth or in the cruise of the Great White Fleet, the advertising exceeded the product. . . .

In reaching decisions about what he took to be wise and possible for the country both at home and abroad Roosevelt relied primarily upon his own intuitive judgments; but he took great pains to base these judgments upon information derived from other sources, notably from those equipped with special knowledge. He sought to obtain, on any given problem, the full spectrum of expert opinion before making up his mind. This is certainly in character. The executive who has no great faith in a body of principled theory as a guide to action must find assistance somewhere and where, more naturally, than in the minds of well-informed men.

A second thing to be extracted from the Roosevelt administration is the feeling for the single man—that man who was to be given as nearly as may be a fair chance to show the stuff that was in him. Roosevelt's instinct for the particular situation, his regard for the intuitive perception, his reliance upon the private scheme of morality all prepared him to look for the individual. He cut down through the dreary classifications of society—the farm vote or the white-collar class —to reach the single man; to snatch the individual from the ranks of cowboys, poets, hunters, mechanics, dukes, bird watchers, politicians, fishermen, publishers, emperors, engineers, wives, and small boys. With individuals from all these ranks and callings Roosevelt set up a direct two-way communication and relationship based on the stuff that was in both him and them. It was not good fellowship; he was in fact a poor good fellow. It was instinctive feeling that only the man himself counts. "While sometimes it is necessary," he wrote in 1900, "from both a legislative and social standpoint, to consider men as a class, yet in the long run our safety lies in recognizing the individual's worth or lack of worth as the chief basis of action, and in shaping our whole conduct, and especially our political conduct, accordingly." It is perhaps strange politics to propose that there are actually unworthy individuals—but it does help to recover for each individual a sense of responsibility for his own worth. How else to measure the stuff that is in you?

This feeling for the individual as opposed to the type springs from a view of nature that assumes that in the conduct of his own affairs man is the measure of all things. It proposes that he must be mindful of himself. This is a moving view of life that has profoundly influenced western culture. Today, in an age that thinks in larger increments— the little people, one third of a nation—this vivid awareness of the individual has a refreshing, and may have a therapeutic, meaning.

Third and last to be considered from these years is an attitude toward power. . . .

It is idle to pretend that this question of authority is not one of man's great perplexities, just as it is idle to pretend that there is not real substance in the Actonian pronouncement. In the past, as it will happen in the future, corrupting influences have burst through the pales and forts of law and morality that have been thrown up around the seats of power. Yet stable social organization must still depend upon applications of authority. Theodore Roosevelt accepted this con- dition of affairs; he believed, he said, in power. Perhaps he believed too much in power, but he was not unaware of its undermining influences. He understood how some able men, like Thomas Collier Platt, were seduced by irresistible desires for control and he knew how other able men, like John Hay, disturbed by the implications of power, thwarted their own energies. In three ways, therefore, he sought to limit the corrupting influence of authority. He looked first to the law—the firmament of ancient custom and current opinion within which the administrator must work. But, though he spoke with respect of the law as a support for character, his respect was qualified. Laws were attempts at uniform solutions, while the specific conflicts in society— varying always in form and intensity—were sometimes better dealt with by executive action unhampered by the generalities of law. So he looked further for other safeguards. He found one in the limiting factor of personal morality, of character, the control of power by the control of self. . . .

. . . In another episode—not so tiny—Roosevelt set up his private system of morality and his own desires against the usages of nations and the morality of other men when, as he said, he took the Canal Zone. There are arguments for him and against him in his behavior here—arguments that have already been put forward with sufficient indignation, humor, or understanding by others. The fact remains that he did indeed take the Canal Zone. For this he would never conceiv- ably apologize, because he thought his action necessary. But he recog- nized the dangers of this attitude in himself and others. He therefore sought one final safeguard—to limit power by limiting its duration. When he told Trevelyan he was for a strong executive he also told him he was not for a perpetual executive. In 1904 he applied this theory specifically to the United States. "A wise custom," he wrote,

". . . limits the President to two terms," and four years later the time came for him to apply the theory specifically to himself. . . .

And so, against the conviction that he was better equipped than anyone else available, against the general clamor of the crowd and the organized pressure of the loyal and the ambitious, against the enchantment cast by power over the man who holds it, Roosevelt put the Presidency by for a season. Reckoned in purely personal terms, the decision of that spring was moving. It seems obvious from his letters that he was wholly tempted and half persuaded to continue while he remained fully convinced that he must make an end of it. . . .

These distinguishing characteristics of the Roosevelt administration —the intuitive approach to situations, the selection of the individual as the primary object of concern in society, the unruffled attitude toward power—were not the exclusive property of Theodore Roosevelt. . . . If one tries to bring these characteristics within a single classification one is tempted, with some reservations and immeasurable trepidation, to say that they are part of the conservative temper, or at least that they are among the primary conservative virtues.

John M. Blum:
President and People

Roosevelt, the heroic image of the constituency he wished, the active "man of intellect," "sound, morally, mentally and physically," captured the loyalty of the people as had no incumbent President since Andrew Jackson.[7] His policies and the devices of leadership by which he made them the law of the land had of themselves constructive purpose. Yet the man and his policies, taken together, had also an appeal which was, as he meant it to be, a vital ingredient in his political effort. Roosevelt was never a mere sounding board for the popular mind. He had, rather, in his halcyon days, an absolute sense of political pitch. He struck the notes that the chorus awaited. This he did intuitively, for he contained within him the best and the worst of America, the whole spectrum from practical enlightenment and sound moral judgment to sentimentalism and braggadocio. He could touch greatness and he could skirt cheapness. . . .

"Common sense, courage and common honesty," buttressed with the fervent pleas for motherhood that Roosevelt issued with righteous repetition, colored his platform with the splendor of Bryan's revivalist imagery. It was, after all, part of the national faith to believe in the "Square Deal" even before Roosevelt so named it. Roosevelt had, moreover, before he stumped the land, herded cattle, captured outlaws, been a kind of policeman, and—single-handed—killed a Spaniard. Not even an urban childhood, myopia, a Harvard degree, a few published books, and tea with Henry Adams damaged those incomparable qualifications. Between the war with Spain and the war in Europe the average American boy, discarding the log cabin and the split rail, adopted a new model of successful conduct—a model that his father, however he voted, cheered throatily and his mother, however she worshiped, endorsed. Even the most partisan, most loyal supporter of Woodrow Wilson confessed unashamed when Roosevelt died that America had loved him.

The "farmers, small businessmen and upper-class mechanics," Roosevelt's "natural allies," in 1904 cheered his deeds as well as the man. . . .

This was the particular genius of Theodore Roosevelt: to achieve dramatically those ends he valued and thereby, often without any but

[7] John Morton Blum, *The Republican Roosevelt* (Cambridge: Harvard University Press, 1954), pp. 55–56, 60–61. Copyright 1954 by the President and Fellows of Harvard College. Reprinted with the permission of the publisher.

an intuitive, unconscious purpose, to increase his political capital. Roosevelt had defined for himself an imprecise line between the "lunatic fringe" he detested and the "selfish rich" he despised. Equally to each of these extremes he was anathema. To many wholly sane but more impatient reformers he seemed insincere. To the inert he seemed mad. Most of early-century America, however, agreed with or at least voted for his Square Deal. This was of course his intention, yet he also intended that the salvation of America was to be justice to all classes. Roosevelt made no secret of this even when he was trying to identify Hanna with the "whole Wall Street crowd." Explaining the purpose of one speech he made at that time, the President wrote: "I wished the labor people absolutely to understand that I set my face like flint against violence and lawlessness of any kind on their part, just as much as against arrogant greed by the rich. . . ."

Odysseus-like, Roosevelt had long steered between the Scylla and Charybdis he here again identified. The convictions of his youth had charted his continuous course. His jagged dread of violent revolution, his aristocrat's disdain for the hauteur of wealth newly won, fixed at any time his safe position. But surest of all, by politics he found his way. He preached partly by instinct, partly by design, what the self-conscious middle class, a safe majority, believed. Thereby he attended not only his own career but also the classic mission of politics, the peaceful reconciliation of conflicting interests.

Since the farmers, the mechanics, and the small businessmen, during the four decades before Roosevelt became President, had received too often something less than justice, he had, in order to balance the national scales, frequently to be their champion. At no time did he propose to push the scales past the point of equilibrium, but simply to reach equilibrium he adopted in his first term those positive policies toward labor and corporations with which the Square Deal is associated. Consequently he expected "the criminal rich and the fool rich" to "do all they can to beat me." Doubtless he overestimated their response. Without tipping the scales in the other direction, without sponsoring either radical unionism or the closed shop, without indiscriminately busting every trust, he expected those he helped to rally to his side. Many of them did.

Howard K. Beale:
Imperialist and Diplomatist

In other hands his ability, his understanding of international problems, his interest in power, his desire to be strong enough to settle questions by might, his secret, highly personal handling of foreign affairs might have become dangerous to democracy and to the peace of the world.[8] What was it that restrained Roosevelt and prevented his becoming dangerous? The democratic process with the chance to criticize government and to retire a leader from public office in the next election provides, of course, an important safeguard that is none the less somewhat offset by the President's power to put the country into war situations where the people would have to support the President however much they deplored his action. Roosevelt's own personal qualities, however, also prevented his use of power from becoming the threat the same power might have been in other hands. In part, Roosevelt was held back by a deep-seated concern about the well-being of his country, and in part by his cautious middle-of-the-road approach to all questions. Furthermore, to a considerable extent, it was the same American aristocratic background that gave him independence and freedom from ordinary social pressures that also restrained him. This background had given him a keen sense of the dignity of man and of the worth of the individual that was never acquired by the mid-century totalitarian rulers with the power he sometimes aspired to. His background, too, had given him a sense of social responsibility and above all an attitude of *noblesse oblige* that dominated him always. Too, he believed thoroughly in America and hence respected the American democratic tradition. And as part of that democratic tradition he respected public opinion. Though he was often frustrated by the inability or unwillingness of the public to see things as he did, still he conceived his role as a democratic head of state to be one of leading public opinion where he could, and yielding where he could not persuade until such time when able leadership like his would be able to persuade. Even in his secret handling of foreign affairs he sometimes refrained from actions he deemed wise, such as formally joining the Anglo-Japanese Alliance, when he felt he would not be able to carry public opinion with him

[8] Howard K. Beale, *Theodore Roosevelt and the Rise of America to World Power* (Baltimore, 1956), pp. 453–54, 456–57, 461–62. Copyright 1956 by the Johns Hopkins Press. Reprinted by permission of the publisher.

when he made his action known. His belief that progress could be achieved by persuading people through democratic processes was in itself part of the Western World's nineteenth-century democratic tradition and at the same time an effective restraint upon the abuse of power.

Indeed, he believed that popular support was as necessary as executive firmness and armed might. Roosevelt had no intention of being left unable to support strong words in foreign policy because the people would not back him. Better no strong words than strong words the people would not stand behind. A foreign policy that the voters would not approve in deeds was as bad as bluffing about something the executive lacked the intention or the power to carry out. Roosevelt never forgot that public opinion was important to successful foreign policy. Hence he devoted much time to creating public support for his policies. He was successful in stimulating in many of the people pride in the new imperial role he envisaged for America. He prepared the way for future comprehension of America's involvement in world affairs. . . .

In the end, for all his activity, his tremendous influence on foreign policy, his surprising insights and prophecies, Roosevelt failed in his most important objectives. He strove to create a stable world in which the great civilized nations would refrain from war upon one another. Yet in less than a decade after his much-heralded success at Portsmouth and his earnest efforts at Algeciras and The Hague, these "civilized" powers were at each other's throats in a gigantic struggle that was to destroy much of what he believed in and to prepare the way for a second world war that was to destroy much more. By balancing Russia against Japan in Manchuria and North China, without letting either one get strong enough to dominate, he believed he was creating a stable Far East open to the trade of all nations. Yet within three years of the Portsmouth Conference the two powers had combined to exclude all other imperial nations. He hoped he had created stability in China by preventing its partition and setting up large-power control over that nation. Yet during much of the next generation China was torn by internal strife and forty years after he left the White House China was to fall under domination by Russia that was to exclude all the powers except Russia. By building American naval power he planned to provide a safe future for his country, since no nation would dare attack her. Yet thirty years after his death, with military might such as his wildest dreams could not have pictured, and with a navy more powerful than any other, his country had suffered losses in battle as great as ever before in its history and was living armed to the teeth in dread of destruction of her cities in an atomic war. He thought he had prepared the way for a century of the "English-speaking" man, and yet by the middle of that century Britain had lost much of her empire and was struggling desperately for survival. . . .

. . . One comes away from the study with admiration for Roosevelt's ability, his energy, and his devotion to his country's interests as he saw them, but with a sense of tragedy that his abilities were turned toward imperialism and an urge for power, which were to have consequences so serious for the future. Perhaps Roosevelt and his friends could not have led America along a different path. In so far, however, as they did influence America's course, they influenced it in a direction that by the mid-century was to bring her face to face with grave dangers. Roosevelt probably had as much ability and handled foreign policy as well as any other statesman of his day. The trouble lay not in his abilities, but in his values and in the setting in which he worked, whether from choice or from necessity.

George E. Mowry:
Broker of the Possible

Theodore Roosevelt was so many things to so many men because he was also many things to himself.[9] The trouble was that the emotional and the intellectual man refused to add up to any round and consistent sum. Many of his dominant impulses were matched by their opposites. But instead of creating an equilibrium within the man, these antipodal feelings sometimes impelled him to go hurtling off, first in one direction and then in another. Roosevelt loved life in all of its phases with a ferocious intensity, and he was not so constituted that he could enjoy any portion of it as a bystander. The quip about him at a wedding that he wanted to be the preacher, the bride, and the bridegroom revealed more possibly than the quipster understood. Roosevelt once remarked that man's mission in life could be summed up with the words "work, fight, and breed." A natural competitor and combatant, he was happiest when testing his powers against those of other men or of the universe. Killing a grizzly bear with a hunting knife, he wrote about a prospective hunting trip, "would be great sport." Yet despite this love for the strenuous life Roosevelt had yearnings for the quieter career of science and scholarship. His first ambition was to be a naturalist. He produced more than one creditable work of history, and at times thought of being a professor. His favorite American Presidents showed something of the cleavage within the man. On the one hand he admired the reflective, compromising, and patient Abraham Lincoln, on the other the impetuous, headstrong, and trigger-quick Andrew Jackson. . . .

Measured against the world-wide socialism of today perhaps Roosevelt was a conservative. What American statesman would not be? But in the context of American history and of his own times his conservatism, to say the least, was a most peculiar type. So was that of his political supporters, the farmers, the small businessman, and the upper-class mechanics. If occasionally he felt a horror of extremes, that did not stop him at other times from going a long way toward the polar positions when public ends and personal ambition were pushing him. If at times he criticized radicals, he was also vociferous in his criticism of conservatives. The truth is that Roosevelt, the politician, often called himself a conservative when he was going in a radical direction

[9] George E. Mowry, *The Era of Theodore Roosevelt, 1900–1912* (New York, 1958), pp. 110, 113–15. Copyright 1958 by George E. Mowry. Reprinted by permission of Harper & Row, Publishers, Inc. The footnotes in the original have been omitted.

and a radical when he was headed the opposite way. Likewise, when writing to his more conservative friends, he was a conservative, and to his more progressive supporters he was a progressive. To the middle he was usually the practical man dealing in justice.

However traditional his code of personal morality, Roosevelt was far more libertarian in other areas. His preference for functionalism and simplicity in public architecture was far advanced for his day and in sharp contrast to the traditional taste for structures after the Greco-Roman mode. If a building was functional but lacked distinction, he wrote, it was at least "never ridiculous" as were some of the copies of old-world castles which dotted the American pioneer earth. . . .

Whether Roosevelt was a conservative or a radical depends largely upon one's yardstick, and how one measures the man. His intellect and emotions were often at odds. So were his deeds and words. In some things he was a traditionalist and in others a reformer. Most of his beliefs and prejudices reflected the beliefs and prejudices of the middle register of Americans, and in that sense he was a progressive. But most of all he was a skillful broker of the possible, a broker between the past and the present, between the interest groups pushing the government one way and the other, between his own conscience and his opportunities. An able, ambitious nondoctrinaire, a moralist with a deep love for his country and an abiding sense of responsibility, he was of that *genus sui generis,* a democratic politician.

Gabriel Kolko:
Friend of Big Business

Roosevelt never ceased to maintain an incurable confidence that institutional reform could best be obtained by personal transformation of evildoers.[10] He found, in the course of the many movements for legislative change, that the members of the press and the public wanted morality imposed on railroads, packers, and others. His response was pragmatic and contemptuous. He worked with reformers if it suited his purposes, but he virtually regarded them as the cause of evils by their consciousness of them. Roosevelt preferred to solve problems by ignoring them, and rarely took leadership during the earliest stages of discussion of industrial or political problems if it was led by those not in his class. Circumstances often forced him to intrude into affairs after intervention could no longer be avoided—he was, after all, conscious of votes and public pressures. But he never questioned the ultimate good intentions and social value of the vast majority of businessmen, nor did he ever attack an obvious abuse in business or take a stand on regulation without discreetly couching his terms with luxuriant praise for the basic economic status quo and the integrity of businessmen.

Nothing better illustrates Roosevelt's fundamental dislike of non-business reformers than his position on the "muckrakers." Exposé literature of the time was, admittedly, often careless and exaggerated, but it was also usually conservative in its motives, and for the most part avoided posing radical alternatives to existing evils. The invidious term "muckraker" was invented by Roosevelt in the midst of the agitation for food, meat, and railroad regulation, causes with which Roosevelt presumably identified himself. On April 14, 1906, Roosevelt made the headlines by attacking "the man with the muck-rake, the man who could look no way but downward . . . who was offered a celestial crown for his muck-rake, but would neither look up nor regard the crown . . . but continued to rake to himself the filth of the floor." Translated into concrete analogies, the celestial crown was apathy and ignorance of the reality about him, a placid, optimistic complacency toward the world as it stood. In the same speech Roosevelt hinted that it might be theoretically desirable to someday have federal income

[10] Gabriel Kolko, *The Triumph of Conservatism: A Reinterpretation of American History, 1900–1916* (Glencoe, Ill., 1963), pp. 111–12, 129. Copyright 1963 by The Free Press of Glencoe. Reprinted by permission of the Macmillan Company. The footnotes in the original have been omitted.

taxation, but in the context of his attack on reformers his innuendo was not taken seriously, and Roosevelt never acted upon it.

Roosevelt was quite sincere in his criticism of the exposé writers. These journalists—Norman Hapgood, Osward Garrison Villard, and especially David Graham Phillips—were the "friend of disorder." "Of course," he confessed to William Allen White, "in any movement it is impossible to avoid having some people go with you temporarily whose reasons are different from yours and may be very bad indeed. Thus in the beef packing business I found that Sinclair was of real use. I have an utter contempt for him. He is hysterical, unbalanced, and untruthful. Three-fourths of the things he said were absolute falsehoods. For some of the remainder there was only a basis of truth." Roosevelt's thoroughly contemptuous attitude toward reformers indicates that their relevations were hardly enough to move him. Support by important business elements was always the decisive factor.

La Follette, of all the contemporary reformers, especially aroused Roosevelt's ire. He is "a shifty self-seeker," Roosevelt told William Allen White in 1906; "an entirely worthless Senator," he concluded several years later. La Follette, for his part, condemned Roosevelt's "equally drastic attack upon those who were seeking to reform abuses. These were indiscriminately classed as demagogues and dangerous persons. In this way he sought to win approval, both from the radicals and conservatives. This cannonading, first in one direction and then in another, filled the air with noise and smoke, which confused and obscured the line of action, but, when the battle cloud drifted by and quiet was restored, it was always a matter of surprise that so little had really been accomplished." La Follette was wrong, of course. A great deal was accomplished, but for conservative ends. . . .

Roosevelt's interpretation of the trust problem, his association of the evils of concentration with the personality of individuals, and his separation of "good" from "bad" combinations as a means of accepting the major premises of the corporate economy, were all part of the dominant thought of the day. His basic ideas, which were virtually identical to the attitude on the "trust problem" taken by the big business supporters of the National Civic Federation, were eminently acceptable to the corporate elite. The idea of federal incorporation or licensing was attractive as a shield against state regulation, and rather than frightening big business, as most historians believe they did, Roosevelt's statements encouraged them. Indeed, even his passing reference in his 1906 Message to Congress to the theoretical desirability of an income tax law was hardly radical. Andrew Carnegie was also attacking the unequal distribution of weath as "one of the crying evils of our day," and the fact that Roosevelt took no concrete steps on the matter, and linked it with a Constitutional amendment, meant his rhetoric was not frightening even to reactionaries.

William H. Harbaugh:
The Roosevelt Legacy

Like most men of heroic proportions, Theodore Roosevelt had made major blunders and miscalculations.[11] He had suffered an acute and far-ranging vision to be blurred by a too sweeping commitment to force or the threat of force. He had blinded himself, except in the memorable year of his Bull Moose heresy, to the moral limitations imposed on his party by its hostage to the men and values of the market place. He had repelled men who should have taken him seriously by his boyish enthusiasms and matchless lust for life. And he had often conveyed the impression of opportunism by the ease with which he had shifted causes and allegiances in the harsh conviction that politics is the art of the possible.

Yet, as in all generalizations about this extraordinary man, the need to qualify and elaborate remains. If Roosevelt the conservative retained to the end a Burkean fear of revolution, Roosevelt the progressive had proclaimed from the beginning a democratic functionalism that was grounded in almost fuller faith in man—in his free moral capacity, his educability, and his power to act finally with disinterest —than Jefferson's. No great American statesman has ever been more committed to an open society based on talent; no American President has ever flirted more seriously with majority rule. Nor, paradoxically, has any major American political leader ever reposed greater confidence in government by experts; nor, still more paradoxically, expounded so emphatically a philosophy of moral absolutes.

If, in the summing up, Roosevelt indulged too indiscriminately in platitudes, as surely he did, and if he extolled character at the sacrifice of depth and breadth of mind, as conservatives have immemorially done, his preachments are nonetheless viable. It is true that they rested on nothing more substantial than his own intuition and intelligence —as he once exclaimed when asked how he knew that justice had been done, "Because I did it." And it is also true that although this was well enough for him, the intuition being deep and the intelligence penetrating, it was not enough for all the men who subsequently held the office he had himself so distinguished. Men of estimable character with one exception and men of narrow intellectual horizons with some exceptions, only a few of them understood, as the mature Roosevelt

[11] William Henry Harbaugh, *Power and Responsibility: The Life and Times of Theodore Roosevelt* (New York, 1961), pp. 520–22. Copyright 1961 by William Henry Harbaugh. Reprinted by permission of Farrar, Straus and Cudahy.

finally did, that a moralism unsupported by social and economic reality is the most meaningless of platitudes.

For all of that, for all, even, of the relativism of the modern mind, the feeling persists that men of character, if blessed also with depth and breadth of view, will always come to a working consensus as to the nature of justice in a given situation. And if such is in truth the case, the ideal of the morally responsible and duty-conscious citizen that Roosevelt so imbued in the minds of his own generation must live on in those that follow.

Whatever the Colonel's ultimate place in the hearts of his countrymen—and it yearly grows larger and warmer—there is no discounting those incisive perceptions and momentous actions that made him such a dynamic historical force from his civil service years to the day of his death. In an age when the excesses of the profit system were undermining the moral foundations of American society, when one great body of reformers was invoking the antiquated ways of the agrarian order and another was uncritically accepting a mechanistic interpretation of man himself, when two of the nation's most ripened historical minds, Brooks and Henry Adams, were evolving theories that closed the ring on all hope, Roosevelt the practical idealist was molding the new determinism and the old individualism into the only synthesis compatible with the American political temperament; the only program that offers hope that industrialism will ultimately serve American society for good rather than ill. Eschewing laissez-faire capitalism no less than doctrinaire socialism, he saw with the pragmatist's genius that "Ruin faces us if we . . . permit ourselves to be misled by any empirical or academic consideration into refusing to exert the common power of the community where only collective action can do what individualism has left undone, or can remedy the wrongs done by an unrestricted and ill-regulated individualism." More, perhaps, than anything else, it was the coincidence of that insight and Roosevelt's disposition to act that explains his dramatic and exhilarating impact on his times.

Long after the rationalizations, the compromises, the infights, the intolerance and all the rest have been forgotten, Theodore Roosevelt will be remembered as the first great President-reformer of the modern industrial era—the first to concern himself with the judiciary's massive property bias, with the maldistribution of wealth, and with the subversion of the democratic process by businessmen and their spokesmen in Congress, the pulpits and the editorial offices; the first to comprehend the conservation problem in its multiple facets, the first to evolve a broad regulatory program for capital, and the first to encourage, however cautiously, the growth of countervailing labor unions; the first President, in fine, to understand and react constructively to the challenge to existing institutions raised by the technological revolution.

And if, for the affront his militarism and chauvinism gave the human spirit, he will never be truly revered as is Lincoln, he will yet for his unique personal qualities and remarkably constructive achievements, among them the realistic pursuit of peace in a world that he understood better than most, be greatly loved and profoundly respected.

Dewey W. Grantham:
Roosevelt and the Historians

One of the notable characteristics of Rooseveltian historiography since World War II is the change in attitude of historians toward Roosevelt.[12] In a recent reference to new works on Roosevelt, Hermann Hagedorn observed that in none of them was there "a trace of the patronizing, even sneering skepticism of the appraisals that had been accepted by too many of the historical writers of the past thirty years as the proper attitude to take toward Mr. Roosevelt. . . ." In many respects this is a desirable development. The older views of Roosevelt associated with Pringle's interpretation and the 1930's surely went too far in picturing the Rough Rider as a political opportunist, a man lacking in principle, and a pseudo-progressive who failed to comprehend the nature of the fundamental problems of his day, evaded issues, and in many ways actually hindered genuine reform. Yet it is a cause for wonder and perhaps concern that, with some important exceptions, most Roosevelt writers since 1945 have not paid proper tribute to the critical side of Clio's craft. Many of these authors have been amateurs, but the lack of critical judgment has also characterized the work on Roosevelt by some professional historians. One need not oppose a proper recognition of Roosevelt's constructive work and prophetic insights to feel that historians and biographers have swung too far away from the skeptical approach of the prewar scholars.

Roosevelt continues to be a controversial figure. His interpreters have not agreed, for example, whether to call him a conservative or a liberal. Although most recent writers have been inclined to accept John M. Blum's characterization of him as an enlightened conservative, two of the leading Roosevelt students—Howard K. Beale and George E. Mowry—have entered dissents and argue that Roosevelt falls within the American liberal tradition. It may well be, as Samuel P. Hays has suggested, that Roosevelt's biographers and historians of the progressive period have been overly concerned with the traditional theme of liberal-conservative conflict. Hays believes that Roosevelt is difficult to characterize because historians have asked the wrong question about him. They have insisted on interpreting the significance of his career as primarily in its role in the social conflict of the late

[12] Dewey W. Grantham, Jr., "Theodore Roosevelt in American Historical Writing, 1945–1960," *Mid-America*, XLIII (January, 1961), 33–35. Reprinted by permission of the author. The footnotes in the original have been omitted.

nineteenth and early twentieth centuries between the business community and the farmer-labor groups. Actually, Hays declares, Roosevelt sought to avoid social struggle, refused to become identified with either side, and is chiefly significant for the attempt he made to supplant this conflict with a "scientific" approach to social and economic questions. Whether or not Theodore Roosevelt was a progressive, it is difficult to disagree with Henry F. May's conclusion that he was "the greatest spokesman of practical idealism in America" and "a compelling symbol of the country's regeneration."

There is much to be said for the historical writing on Theodore Roosevelt during the years 1945–1960. Far better than was true before 1945, recent scholars, most notably John M. Blum, have illuminated the roots of Roosevelt's career and the sources of his convictions. There is now, after George E. Mowry's excellent work, a new understanding of the impetus the twenty-sixth President gave to progressive politics in the United States, and of his own evolving progressivism. His skill in the game of politics, his contribution to the revivification of the presidency, his awareness of the implications of America's new industrial society and his efforts to work out policies for adjusting to it, his understanding of the fact that the United States was, inexorably, a part of the world and her foreign policy must be shaped with that in mind —all of these things about Roosevelt have become much clearer during the last decade and a half. Meanwhile, scores of historians not directly concerned with Roosevelt have helped to fill in the historical interstices of his period. And, finally, recent Rooseveltian historiography has suggested, even if it has not adequately explained, those defects in Roosevelt's character and those limitations in his policies which prevented him from being an even greater American.

Bibliographical Note

The printed materials for a study of Theodore Roosevelt are extensive. Two collections of his own writings are indispensable for the serious student: Hermann Hagedorn, ed., *The Works of Theodore Roosevelt*, National Edition, 20 vols. (New York, 1926), and Elting E. Morison and associates, ed., *The Letters of Theodore Roosevelt*, 8 vols. (Cambridge, 1951–54). *The Works* contain TR's books and important articles, as well as his major state papers and a selection of his many speeches. The last volume includes his *Autobiography*, a classic first published in 1913 and a convenient summary of the twenty-sixth president's basic ideas. *The Letters* bring together about 6,500 of the more than 100,000 Roosevelt letters in the Library of Congress. These publications provide an easily accessible and invaluable record of Roosevelt's thought and action. His addresses and messages as president can be found in *Presidential Addresses and State Papers*, 8 vols. (New York, 1910) and in Volumes X and XI of James D. Richardson, ed., *A Compilation of the Messages and Papers of the Presidents, 1789–1909*, 11 vols. (New York, 1911). William H. Harbaugh, ed., *The Writings of Theodore Roosevelt* (Indianapolis, 1967), is an excellent one-volume anthology. For other useful selections from Roosevelt's own works, see Farida A. Wiley, ed., *Theodore Roosevelt's America: Selections from the Writings of the Oyster Bay Naturalist* (New York, 1955), and Hermann Hagedorn, comp. and ed., *The Theodore Roosevelt Treasury: A Self-Portrait from His Writings* (New York, 1957).

The newspapers and periodicals of Roosevelt's generation reveal in abundant measure how fully he caught the imagination of his contemporaries. He was also the subject of a large number of books and memoirs by those who knew him and observed his strenuous activities at first hand. Among these are John Burroughs, *Camping & Tramping with Roosevelt* (Boston, 1907) ; Albert Shaw, ed., *A Cartoon History of Roosevelt's Career* (New York, 1910); Lawrence F. Abbott, *Impressions of Theodore Roosevelt* (Garden City, 1919); William Roscoe Thayer, *Theodore Roosevelt: An Intimate Biography* (Boston, 1919); William W. Sewall, *Bill Sewall's Story of T.R.* (New York, 1919); William Draper Lewis, *The Life of Theodore Roosevelt* (Philadelphia, 1919); Joseph Bucklin Bishop, *Theodore Roosevelt and His Time Shown in His Own Letters*, 2 vols. (New York, 1920); Lawrence F. Abbott, ed., *The Letters of Archie Butt, Personal Aide to President Roosevelt* (Garden City, 1924); Oscar King Davis, *Released for Publication: Some Inside Political History of Theodore Roosevelt and His Times, 1898–1918*

(Boston, 1925); and Owen Wister, *Roosevelt: The Story of a Friendship, 1880–1919* (New York, 1930). Three members of Roosevelt's family have characterized him in memoirs: Corinne Roosevelt Robinson, *My Brother Theodore Roosevelt* (New York, 1921); *Day Before Yesterday: The Reminiscences of Mrs. Theodore Roosevelt, Jr.* (Garden City, 1959); and Nicholas Roosevelt, *Theodore Roosevelt: The Man as I Knew Him* (New York, 1967).

Other memoirs that throw light on TR are *The Autobiography of William Allen White* (New York, 1946); Gifford Pinchot, *Breaking New Ground* (New York, 1947); and Booker T. Washington, *My Larger Education* (New York, 1911). For critical appraisals by contemporaries, see Robert M. La Follette, *La Follette's Autobiography: A Personal Narrative of Political Experiences* (Madison, Wis., 1913); Amos R. E. Pinchot, *History of the Progressive Party, 1912–1961,* ed. Helene Maxwell Hooker (New York, 1958); and Oswald Garrison Villard, *Fighting Years: Memoirs of a Liberal Editor* (New York, 1939).

The most comprehensive and reliable one-volume biography of the twenty-sixth president is William Henry Harbaugh's *Power and Responsibility: The Life and Times of Theodore Roosevelt* (New York, 1961), an authoritative and fair-minded work. Henry F. Pringle's mocking and disparaging study, *Theodore Roosevelt: A Biography* (New York, 1931), still merits inclusion in a Roosevelt bibliography. A brilliant narrative, sprinkled with insights into the character and mentality of the boisterous "Teddy," it was the most significant and durable contribution by the debunking school to Rooseveltian literature. Indispensable for an understanding of Roosevelt is John Morton Blum's slender volume, *The Republican Roosevelt* (Cambridge, 1954). This influential interpretation pictures TR as a skillful conservative and does a great deal to clarify "the purposes and methods" of his career. Another discerning and sophisticated interpretation is G. Wallace Chessman's *Theodore Roosevelt and the Politics of Power* (Boston, 1969). In *The Seven Worlds of Theodore Roosevelt* (New York, 1958), Edward Wagenknecht tries with some success to distill the essence of Roosevelt's thought and to delineate the character of his leadership. A popular biography by Noel F. Busch, *T.R.: The Story of Theodore Roosevelt and His Influence on Our Times* (New York, 1963), offers a sympathetic and undocumented modern account. Hermann Hagedorn's *The Roosevelt Family of Sagamore Hill* (New York, 1954) is a warm and entertaining account of the Roosevelt family at its Long Island home. Stefan Lorant's *The Life and Times of Theodore Roosevelt* (Garden City, 1959) assembles a large number of pictures, cartoons, diaries, and letters in an effort to recapture the Colonel's "life" and "times."

Despite the scholarly attention Roosevelt has received during the last quarter-century, he still awaits comprehensive treatment at the hands of a single biographer. Carleton Putnam has projected a four-volume biography, but has published only the first volume. This readable and well-documented work, *Theodore Roosevelt: The Formative Years, 1858–1886* (New York, 1958), represents the most detailed study yet made of TR's youth and early career. In addition, a large number of monographs and specialized accounts are concerned with aspects of Roosevelt's life and public service. The most notable contribution of this kind is George E. Mowry's *Theodore Roosevelt and the Progressive Movement* (Madison, Wis., 1946), a perspicacious and well-written treatment of Roosevelt's influence on the progressive movement and the influence of the movement on the man. More recently, G. Wallace Chessman has published an important study of Roosevelt's governorship, *Governor Theodore Roosevelt: The Albany Apprenticeship, 1898–1900* (Cambridge, 1965). This book illuminates Roosevelt's relations with the legislature and with Boss Platt and helps explain the complicated political situation in New York near the end of the century. Howard Lawrence Hurwitz offers a critical appraisal of Roosevelt's labor policies in *Theodore Roosevelt and Labor in New York State, 1880–1900* (New York, 1943). Another critical view is presented in an older and somewhat neglected study by Richard Cleveland Baker, *The Tariff under Roosevelt and Taft* (Hastings, Neb., 1941). Roosevelt's life as a rancher is dealt with by Hermann Hagedorn in *Roosevelt in the Bad Lands* (Boston, 1921), while his embodiment of the western theme is explored in a significant new volume by G. Edward White, *The Eastern Establishment and the Western Experience: The West of Frederic Remington, Theodore Roosevelt, and Owen Wister* (New Haven, 1968). Paul Russell Cutright's *Theodore Roosevelt the Naturalist* (New York, 1956) is an interesting study of Roosevelt's outdoor life by a zoologist.

Among the many volumes that focus on Theodore Roosevelt's conduct of foreign relations, the most valuable is Howard K. Beale's *Theodore Roosevelt and the Rise of America to World Power* (Baltimore, 1956). This monograph, vigorously written and based on exhaustive research, is a comprehensive and critical examination of TR's policies in the international sphere. David H. Burton's *Theodore Roosevelt: Confident Imperialist* (Philadelphia, 1969) is a revealing study of Roosevelt's imperialist thought. In his *Ideals and Self-Interest in America's Foreign Relations: The Great Transformation of the Twentieth Century* (Chicago, 1953), Robert E. Osgood sees Roosevelt as a symbol in the conflict between ideals and self-interest in American foreign relations during the first two decades of the twentieth century. Roosevelt's handling of Japanese-American relations is the subject of three good books: Raymond A. Esthus, *Theodore Roosevelt and Japan*

(Seattle, 1966); Charles E. Neu, *An Uncertain Friendship: Theodore Roosevelt and Japan, 1906–1909* (Cambridge, 1967); and Thomas A. Bailey, *Theodore Roosevelt and the Japanese-American Crises: An Account of the International Complications Arising from the Race Problem on the Pacific Coast* (Stanford, 1934). Two older monographs that are still of some value are Tyler Dennett, *Roosevelt and the Russo-Japanese War: A Critical Study of American Policy in Eastern Asia in 1902–5, Based Primarily upon the Private Papers of Theodore Roosevelt* (Garden City, 1925), and Howard C. Hill, *Roosevelt and the Caribbean* (Chicago, 1927). For a concise and competent treatment of Roosevelt's contributions to the building of the modern American navy, consult Gordon Carpenter O'Gara, *Theodore Roosevelt and the Rise of the Modern Navy* (Princeton, 1943).

Examples of the many interpretive essays on Roosevelt are William Allen White, *Masks in a Pageant* (New York, 1928) ; John Chamberlain, *Farewell to Reform: The Rise, Life and Decay of the Progressive Mind in America* (New York, 1932); Louis Filler, *Crusaders for American Liberalism* (New York, 1939); Dixon Wecter, *The Hero in America* (New York, 1941); Hamilton Basso, *Mainstream* (New York, 1943); Richard Hofstadter, *The American Political Tradition and the Men Who Made It* (New York, 1948); Peter R. Levin, *Seven by Chance: The Accidental Presidents* (New York, 1948); Daniel Aaron, *Men of Good Hope: A Story of American Progressives* (New York, 1951); Charles A. Madison, *Leaders and Liberals in 20th Century America* (New York, 1961); and Richard Lowitt, "Theodore Roosevelt," in Morton Borden, ed., *America's Ten Greatest Presidents* (Chicago, 1961).

The best general account of the Roosevelt presidency is George E. Mowry's *The Era of Theodore Roosevelt, 1900–1912* (New York, 1958). Other works that throw light on the Roosevelt administration are Harold U. Faulkner, *The Quest for Social Justice, 1898–1914* (New York, 1931) ; Matthew Josephson, *The President Makers: The Culture of Politics and Leadership in an Age of Enlightenment, 1896–1919* (New York, 1940); Mark Sullivan, *Our Times,* 6 vols. (New York, 1926–35), Volumes I–III; and Robert H. Wiebe, *Businessmen and Reform: A Study of the Progressive Movement* (Cambridge, 1962). Among more specialized studies the following are important for an understanding of Roosevelt's activities: Clifford P. Westermeier, *Who Rush to Glory, the Cowboy Volunteers of 1898* . . . (Caldwell, Idaho, 1958); Paul P. Van Riper, *History of the United States Civil Service* (Evanston, Ill., 1958); Samuel P. Hays, *Conservation and the Gospel of Efficiency: The Progressive Conservation Movement, 1890–1920* (Cambridge, 1959); Elmo R. Richardson, *The Politics of Conservation: Crusades and Controversies, 1897–1913* (Berkeley, 1962); Allan Reed Millett, *The Politics of Intervention: The Military Occupation of Cuba, 1906–1909* (Columbus, Ohio, 1968); and Eugene P. Traini, *The Treaty of Portsmouth: An Adventure in American Diplomacy* (Lexington, Ky., 1969).

A useful bibliography of works on Theodore Roosevelt is included in Wagenknecht's *The Seven Worlds of Theodore Roosevelt.* For other bibliographical guides, see Gilbert J. Black, ed., *Theodore Roosevelt, 1858–1919: Chronology-Documents-Bibliographical Aids* (Dobbs Ferry, N.Y., 1969), and the notes in William Henry Harbaugh, *The Life and Times of Theodore Roosevelt* (New York, 1963). Much of the secondary literature is appraised in Dewey W. Grantham, Jr., "Theodore Roosevelt in American Historical Writing, 1945–1960," *Mid-America,* XLIII (January, 1961), 3–35.

Index